NEW YORK CITY
SUBWAY DRAMA,
AND BEYOND

NEW YORK CITY SUBWAY DRAMA, AND BEYOND

MATT LAVELLE

iUniverse, Inc.
Bloomington

NEW YORK CITY SUBWAY DRAMA, AND BEYOND

iUniverse books may be ordered through booksellers or by contacting:

iUniverse
1663 Liberty Drive
Bloomington, IN 47403
www.iuniverse.com
1-800-Authors (1-800-288-4677)

ISBN: 978-1-4620-4441-2 (sc)
ISBN: 978-1-4620-4446-7 (ebk)

Printed in the United States of America

iUniverse rev. date: 08/18/2011

Welcome to the the SUBWAY DRAMA part of my story telling saga. These are all things I have seen personally or have been relayed to me by good friends. Although these stories may seem over the top,. life in the NYC Subway can get just like that. Like when the water just BOILS over on the stove. This is the real NYC that most Tourists will never see. Anytime you head downstairs you enter this secondary world where you are vulnerable to any and all extreme close-ups of the human condition. Conductors have died by not bringing their heads inside fast enough pulling out of the station. One time a man fell in the tracks,. and another man saved his life by jumping in and covering him in the space between the rails as they both got run over!! People have lost limbs getting to close to the edge, Dogs have died. There's the whole thing about an entire community that LIVES down there like the MORLOCKS from the XMEN. (Sometimes I look out the window between stations looking for any sign of life). The Manhattan Transit Authority (MTA),. is big on their own history and even has a museum about how this crazy system,. an actual underground railroad was built. (yeah,. people died digging out Manhattan island for sure.) It's also a corrupt runaway money train that is run like the US government, getting as much money as possible for the people in power while screwing the actual people. The brain never knows, and actually doesn't care what the body is doing. There's Millions of people down there every day,. and that means Millions of dollars going down.

The token booth clerks have an entire culture of their own within the system. When they sold tokens, they were busy cashiers. When the advent of the METROCARD, they became part time cashiers, information providers, and otherwise really bored people stuck behind plastic or plexi glass all day, who I often see bullshitting on the phone like they were at home, or reading a book. (Ive had them get angry at me for interrupting them.) Most often, they have no idea what's going on service wise, or if any drama has one of the lines being jacked up or re-routed,and when asked they will tell you the wrong information with directness and confidence.Many of these folks have spent 20 plus years down there day in and day out.

The Conductors are really to themselves and most of them ignore the people as much as possible.They try to explain where your at and where your going through the intercom,but most of the time it doesn't make any sense,and comes out as either to loud,or to quiet,electronic garble.More than half of them get personally MAD when we hold the doors open,and after we pull out,they deliver a lecture.When they really want us to hear them,suddenly they are loud and clear.RELEASE THE DOORS.RELEASE THE DOOR.WHEN YOU HOLD THE DOORS YOU DELAY THE TRAIN.When your entire life is getting trains to move forward,being slowed down by us,the people,GRATES after awhile.Once the trains are in motion,most will quickly go to their little booths and close the door,cutting themselves off from us,although I've seen some just sit and relax with us like they had nothing to do with the Trains operation.Like the post office,the workers are a Diverse group,filled with minorities,and all of there accents can throw you off.

The cleaning crews are a hardcore lot creeping through the tunnels late at night in gangs,. or otherwise power washing platforms with big water trucks from up on the street.In realms of the upkeep on stations,its real simple:In the money and tourist areas,. they are ON.POINT.Out on the G train in Brooklyn,. they look like abandoned bomb shelters from world war 2 . . .

Here are some appetizers,. the kind of people we may meet along the ride . . .

The guy sitting across from me SMOKING,. which your not allowed to do.Some weird European guy who kept staring at me,and finally saying,.

"I know why your beard is tied in this way.It means you are Black".

The guy wearing a GARBAGE BAG for clothes who REEKS with a smell beyond description,. but what all human beings can reach if they abandon the whole "clean" vibe . . .

"WHAT?! What are you looking at? Want me to come closer? I have what you NEED!"

He said this to me as I was the only other person in the car,and both the front and back doors of the car were locked,and the train was stopped with no explanation.Maybe I had reached hell.

The guy in a PACKED train trying to EAT a chicken salad sandwich with WAY to much chicken salad getting his half eaten food all over me.

"Hey man, . . . want some of my sandwich? It tastes REAL good!."

The woman who I actually FACE LASHED with my backpack straps trying to force my way deeper in the car in a rush . . .

"OW!!,.YOU ASSHOLE . . ."

(I went to the next car)

The kid I "HAT BUMPED", . . . (when your new baseball hat lid head buts an innocent person in the forehead,. HARD,.)

(When the trains go express they can throw you around and force you to hat bump, . . . watch out)

The guy who worked at the post office with 2 giant feather earrings,. standing on the platform,. who when the doors opened up with no room,. grabbed this guys briefcase,(some wall street guy inside the car),and threw it outside on the platform . . .

"Fetch Bitch!" he said.

Wall street guy had no choice and left the train to get his briefcase,. and then feather guy went and stood right where he was:the only room left in the car.

Wall street guy came back as the doors closed in his face,. with feather guy staring and smiling at him through the glass as the train pulled out ... (sweet)

WELCOME to the show folks ... cue:Duke Ellington's song Take the A train,. perfect music to play during our trip through this part of town.

Cant you just hear those rails a hummin?

PICTURE

SUBWAY DRAMA 1

The first Subway drama to come to mind has to be the one that's the most personal for me,. the one where I almost DIED . . . Sometime in 2002.

When I was living in Jackson Heights, . . . I used to get up every day and take a bus to the subway station in Queens to get to Manhattan NYC to my job at Tower records.As a musician,I used to take my horns with me so I could go from work to the gig or rehearsals. This kind of schedule left me tired most of the time.This particular morning I made it to the Roosevelt ave 7 train platform.The 7 is one of the above ground trains,. on a big elevated platform that leads from Manhattan all the way to Shea stadium(the Mets),and Flushing.(where the Nanny lived).

I was more bleary eyed than usual having played 2 gigs the night before,and I was standing,. leaning on my bass clarinet case.TO close to the edge of the tracks,. on the verge of falling asleep waiting for the subway.Obviously not cool.

The train appeared on the horizon,. and like most people in NYC,. I reacted instantly,. you have to be prepared to fight for a seat,and with all the shit I'm carrying,. I want one. My sudden knee-jerk reaction sends my Bass Clarinet right DOWN IN THE FREAKIN' TRACKS . . .

Oh shit . . .

Truth is,. the Bass Clarinet I was carrying around was not a very good one.It was VERY important to me though,. I was working on it every day.It would be hard to replace,. and I

5

would lose progress if I lost it. It also represented something larger to me,. a connection to my music,. and I was in the frame of mind that NYC was not going to defeat me.

So with the train even closer now,. getting louder and closer by the second, . . . I ask myself a quick question,. "Is is to far down? Will I be able to get back up and NOT DIE?" I decided It looked like I could do this myself,. no time to ask for help,. no way to stop the train,. so . . .

DOWN IN THE TRACKS I GO.

I'm not thinking about the THIRD RAIL nearby,. enough electricity to FRY me. I heard the charge come through that means the train is close. ZZZZAAAAASSHHP. To close for comfort now.

As I grab my horn case and throw it up on the platform,. I said out loud, . . . "Got you motherfucker",. and as I turned I saw an older Asian woman looking at me,. pointing and SCREAMING. Whatever I'm doing right now,. it's clearly not part of what is OK in regards to Life itself. The train is PRETTY DAMN CLOSE.

NOT close enough though,. about 20 seconds away,. and I AM able to get back up on the platform.

Whew.

Good thing I was able to climb back up,. since nobody offered any help. A bunch of people look at me like I'm NUTS. The train opens up,. and I get a seat . . . Shit,. disregarding and risking your life deserves a seat,. or at least a smack in the face. The woman that I freaked out is in the same car,. and when she sees me she moves to the other side of the car and then changes cars again at the next stop to get away from me. Who knows what my next act will be?

I would like to say I stopped for a second and thought about what was at stake. Was it stupid? Yeah. Is my life worth that kind of risk? No. I'm an ARIES, . . . we act first, . . . and think later. In fact,. Aries might be the only sign to pull this off,. or Die in the process.

My only explanation,. is that that's how much my music means to me. Its my life,. and in that situation on that day,. I risked it all. I'm not living without it. I've fought to hard and to long to go out on some bullshit. I didn't have enough money to get another bass-clarinet. Plus . . . the way I got that horn in first place to me was pre-ordained in a way. If the train got fucked up and went out of service maybe I could get in some kind of trouble to I thought,. (yeah all lame excuses,. but that's what was in my mind on the way to work)

Kingston NY 1996

I'm on self imposed exile from straight ahead trumpet land in NYC. I'm living with a woman 11 years older than me who had three kids, all young. I start having dreams about bass clarinets where I'm floating inside a giant one,. like a bass clarinet building with no center. I'm in the TONE WORLD,. which sends me to a music store on main st the next day.

"Hey man, . . . you got any used bass-clarinets you want to get rid of? I have about $100."

"As a matter of fact, . . . I do."

SUBWAY DRAMA 2

Down in the subway,. everybody is forced to look at life at lot closer than most of us would want to. Your forced to just be CLOSER with everyone,. and end up interacting with people that if you could,. you would clearly not. The good and bad of life is there for everyone to see. When I say bad,. I also mean the WORST,. and two times the ugly head of RACISM reared it's UGLY head . . . First up,. the BAD . . .

7 train again,. man, . . . did I spend some hours on the one. Supposedly,. the train actually goes UNDER the river which is weird and scary when you think about it. In Between is Roosevelt island,. one stop,. different and less crowded. Somewhere between Grand central,. the last stop in Manhattan and Roosevelt,. 2 African American woman,. early 20's maybe, and a big white guy started having an argument. I was listening but also staying out of it,. like many people. It was clear that they did not know each other. I believe the beef started over the way somebody acted in going for one of the seats. The true EVIL came out shortly before the Roosevelt island stop when the white guy says,. "I've tried to be patient with you 2 Ni****s". (Yes,. the N word,. but I cant bring myself to use it,. that's just me.) I heard him say it,. and was shocked that he came out with it,. no Klan hood, and no confederate flag shit. One of the 2 woman got REALLY Tight,. told the white guy that they would kick his ass for saying that shit,. and more about the possibilities he had now created. She said this as the doors opened up.

Next was truly Evil,. as the white guy pushed both of them out on the platform forcing them into a physical confrontation. He was a big, tall guy,. way bigger than the woman. An older woman inside the train screamed "Call the police!!" (with a thick accent). I didn't see this shit coming and was at a loss,. like most of the people on board,. we were like a dear caught in the headlights. The doors close leaving the trio on the platform as the train pulls out. Right before were out of view I see the white guy grab the woman who was the most vocal and slam her head into the wall. I saw her hold her head and fall to the ground before all I could see was subway wall. Somebody sitting near me told me he was going to report this to the police once we were above ground. I never heard or found out what happened,. and hope the woman survived.

Now,. the light at the end of the tunnel,. as I have a chance to DO something about this kind of Shit,. kind of . . . (this here is the GOOD)

7 train AGAIN. At the end of the 7 in Times square the 7 trains pull in and wait to fill up while the other train comes in. When the other comes in, the other train leaves. I got off work at 5 and would end up on the 7 platform around 5:30,. 5 days a week. (I did this for years). There's almost always a train waiting to go for extended periods here,. so they fill up with passengers. This is when I started running into this guy who had his own routine . . . spreading a message of hate.

Most of the people on the 7 train don't speak English, . . . and this "ultra-America" guy decided he needed to explain to them that they were the lowest form of life on earth, . . . and that they didn't deserve to be in the great USA. From car to car he would go and give a speech in each one, . . . about how all the people there should leave the country right away,. all kinds of racist shit. Ironically, . . . not knowing English was a blessing for the people being attacked, . . . it made the racist guy another crazy rant guy, . . . which most people ignore anyway. He was old,. out of shape,. and was not very clear and articulate to say the least. He never rode the train,. always stepping out before we leave.

After seeing this guy over and over again, . . . and the train being parked, . . . I decided I had had enough of this shit, . . . and much in the way I jumped into the subway tracks, I acted without thinking. What I knew was that in a fight,. I could take this guy,. and part of me wanted to,. having recently watched Fight Club.

So when he next came to the car I was in,. trying to relax with a seat for the trip home after work,. I made my move. I got in this his face,. grabbed him, . . . dragged him and pushed him out onto the subway platform, . . . and told him that this racist shit was over,(among some other choice words).Out on the platform,. I told him that if I saw him again, . . . the same thing would happen again and again.His only response was "Who are you supposed to be?" I was pissed, . . . and in an ARIES state again, . . . this time in confrontation with this tired,tired,tired drama.I didn't hit him or hurt him,. but let him know I was about to,. and actually wanted to.He stayed on the platform and the train left.He stayed quiet,. looked at the ground,and I got on the next train and left.I considered this Case Closed.

About a week later I saw him getting on a 7 train around the same time, . . . and I went to throw him out, . . . again, . . . and then to my surprise, . . . his message had radically changed.

NOW, . . . homeboy was giving out crosses and calling on everyone to come to God.

God loves you was his message, . . . and he made no mention of the threat of hell, . . . no mention of "turn now or suffer for eternity", . . . none of that, . . . now his message was plain and simple, . . . God loves you.He went from car to car.(a sharp contrast to the table set up in the tunnel nearby which gives away free mini comic books that all say if your not with Jesus,. you will burn in hell for eternity).There was no need to throw him out now that his message was LOVE,. so,as self appointed guardian of what is right and what ain't,. I decided to let him be.I saw him notice me out of the corner of his eye.Might as well make sure this isn't a one act play right?

I like to think I had a hand in getting this guy to, . . . if anything, . . . take the simple step of renouncing racism.He could have also just been crazy and bi-polar and I got him to "switch",you never know these days.I don't ride the 7 much anymore, . . . but the last time I was there, . . . I saw this guy still doing his thing.His message was still on point, . . . God is Love.My days as an undercover spiritual subway policeman were over,. and I had a decent action reaction that I proud of.

I was able to at least once,. fight back against something I myself really HATE.

SUBWAY DRAMA 3

At what used to be HELL'S KITCHEN in NYC,. the west side from the Port Authority to Lincoln center,. there are areas where you have like 8 Bodega's (convenience stores run by minorities) within a 2 block radius.(I say used to because Chelsea gets higher every day and soon the whole area will be restaurants and Bars).I lived in this area a long time and still have long term musician friends holding it down.The Bodega's are still holding court,. and seem to do quite well,. usually family run.They were an integral part of my life for years.My favorite was the corner of 50th and 9th,. where I actually hung out with my man AVOCADO.

We had a weird thing though,. in that Avocado was both of our names . . .

One day I asked them for some avocado,. and when they said they were out,. I kept it going. Wait,. how about avocado bread? avocado pie? avocado soda? avocado ice cream?

This one guy was intrigued by the possibility of Avocado ice cream and asked me if it was real . . .

"Hell yeah,. I have that shit every day,. you mean you DON'T carry it?"

"Your crazy man . . .",. my new friend told me,. and from there on in,. whenever I came in,. he would shout Avocado! and put me at the front of the line.I asked him his name,. and he said, . . ."You don't know? its avocado man!", . . .

So we called each other Avocado for years . . .

One time I saw Avs on the street around 3am outside his bodega. He was REALLY Drunk.

He stumbled over to me and said, . . . "aVOcadO, . . . whAT SHoulD i dO wIth aLl THIs mONEy?", . . . and showed me a WAD of Jackson's and that guy that discovered electricity, . . . Franklin or some shit . . .

When I saw how vulnerable he was,. I took him to the bodega,. and the guys put him asleep in the basement . . .

See, . . . I KNOW where this can go, . . . from SUBWAY DRAMA 3:

It's the 1 train going uptown towards Columbia University,. (and eventually Harlem) mid day on a Saturday. Its a brief above ground section,. I remember the Sun.

I'm minding my own business when some Latin American cat,. Yes,. I think He's Mexican,. (Avocado was from Guatemala),. comes up to me very drunk. Drunk enough to pull out and FAN a nice display of hundred dollar bills.

"LoOK.!, . . . LOoK AT ALL ThE MOneY I'VE MAdE."

And than his self celebration begins as he sings to the whole subway car, . . .

"GoD BLeSs AMERicahh,. ! GOD blEss amerICA!!", . . . (still displaying the CASH)

2 young,. street wise characters,. are right across from us, and I can see them ready to POUNCE . . . So I try get this guy to Cool out,.

Under my breath,. and with body language I was like, . . . "man . . . will . . . you . . . chill . . . the . . . fuck . . . out . . ."

We get to the next stop, . . . to late.(sigh) . . .

As the doors open . . . a fluid street ballet of destruction begins,. (please cue:slow motion and opera)

BAM! FIRST GUY JUMPS UP AND PUNCHES MY MAN IN THE SIDE OF THE HEAD

BAM! SECOND GUY GRABS ALL THE MONEY HE WAS HOLDING UP

BAM! THERE OUTSIDE THE PLATFORM AND GONE

BAM! DOORS SEAL,. TRAIN PULLS OUT.

I helped my man up,. he was shocked,and looked at me crying . . . I felt bad,. but what could I do? As usual,. if it doesn't effect us,. we don't respond.Channel 7 has a series about this called "What Would You Do?".The real pain,. the REAL pain,. is mom's that abuse and smack their kids around.Kids are property when that shit goes down.Anyway,. back to my man . . .

"My mOney, . . . my moNey, . . . my monEy" . . .

"I tried to tell you to put it away man".,

I got off in Harlem and could only thing of one thing as I walked away . . .

"Welcome to America" . . .

Some folks get tight when I say that,. but that's what I felt.When people say "America,. Love it or Leave it",. I say . . .

"The way shit is getting,. there's a pretty good case to BOUNCE.

This is the shit I discuss at the SANTERMO pharmacy on 10th between 51st and 52nd.

SUBWAY DRAMA 4

Couples have a unique way of bonding through crazy adversity,. like addiction or being homeless,as shown underground.Folks like:

The METH COUPLE.Spotting somebody on Methadone somewhere along the way with their Heroin addiction is not hard.It's the posture.I've seen these people enter a unique above and below perception where it seems they have no spines! Seriously,. they appear to be aware of where they are,. but enter advanced Yoga positions as they bounce along on the train,. heads WAY between the knees.Seeing couples like this,. (I've only seen the male/female version so far),. they seemingly try to stick together and help each other get high.What's out is watching them try to come out of their delirium to catch the train or something.It takes them awhile.It's difficult to watch,. and I hate to admit it, . . . I've found it to actually be hilarious,. really embarrassing a girlfriend once,. as I just couldn't help laughing watching them.I'm sorry but people sleeping on the train can be funny.I myself once woke up on a crowded 7 train during rush hour leaning forward with my mouth wide open drooling I was so asleep.I'll never forget the look on the 2 Latina's faces when I woke up.

But It's this Homeless couple that really steals the show downstairs,. pull up a seat . . .

It's the 2 express, . . . Pumpin and Bumpin along.Sleep-heads are bouncin',. (This one sleepy guy standing holding the pole better be careful),. and this white couple in their 50's,. looks like there street folks for sure,are also standing with an empty cart.Their relationship is about to reach CRITICAL.MASS.

Their having a serious argument, . . . going back and forth with the man more agitated. The source seemingly being the shopping cart they seem to co-own. It escalates . . .

Man: "I am SO sick and TIRED of this shit. You love this cart more than you love me?"

Woman: "What? not true, . . . your fucking crazy. It's dead. Your alive. I DON'T love it more than you,. I DON'T. (She may be more drunk than the guy,. who "seems",. more lucid.) They have some control power dynamic shit going on in their coupleness.

Man: "Your full of shit, that's a LIE . . . In fact,. I'm gonna squash this once and for all!"

So the man grabs up the cart, . . . and drags it to the space between the cars . . . (Oh Shit,. it's dangerous out there,. what the hell is this nut up to?, . . . were going EXPRESS,. (like 70mph!) The woman tries to stop him, . . . and he forces her off

Woman: "NO . . . STOP . . . What are you doing? She was upset,. but couldn't really get loud,. she pleaded with the man,. not knowing what he had in store . . .

Woman: "PLEASE don't do anything. We need this cart. I LOVE YOU MORE THAN THE CART.

Man: "I DON'T BELIEVE YOU" . . . (As he drags it through the doors),. "I'll show you what happens when you try to get in my way . . .".(OK,. the rest of us on the train are a little uneasy now,. he's taking this shit to far,. what if he throws that shit in the tracks?)

Well we cant see it,. but we sure can HEAR it . . .

SREEEEAKKKK CRASHSSSKKKK.

LOUD AS HELL. I saw SPARKS and shit . . . flashing lights,. almost like special effects . . .

We didn't derail,. but were slowing down. I'm sure the conductor is like WTF? Of course some people start checking their watches,. pissed that this might delay them from whatever mission there on. This could have fucked up the train somehow, . . .

Man returns,. resolute, . . . under his breath, . . . "I . . . told . . . you . . . I . . . told . . . you . . ."

Then it gets DARKER . . . way darker.

Man walks over and punches the woman in the face! She goes down . . .

. . . .

HOLD UP. Now THAT was not cool. The WHOLE vibe changed. The poor woman,. I'll never forget her face lying on her back,. almost like she was in a coffin. She was crying, . . . "why?" I think I heard her say softly . . .

Then before anybody can react,. the cart destroyer leaps to her aid,. helping her up . . .

I'M SORRY! I'M SORRY! I LOVE YOU! I'M SORRY!!

The train limps into the station,. door's open,. and the couple leaves. The man is holding her hand,. and they move quickly.

Man: A little sterner: "Let's get out of here" . . .

END SCENE. (this WAS a true story)

Homeless people get cast aside and judged in general in NYC. They have their own adversity and their very own HUMAN drama. A little bit different, . . . but a being human drama none the less. One could do a whole documentary on homeless folks that use the train to survive.Some just live in the cars and never bathe.Some are straight entertainers.Some people simply have no place else to be.Then there's the folks that live in the TUNNELS. (Special thanks and props to Lord Tubman Antimara.)

SUBWAY DRAMA 5

Many of us have jumped the turnstile at some point, . . . and many of us have been busted. One time I tried to climb over and put my foot on the bar thinking it would hold because I didn't pay. The bar turned,. and I went flying,. landing at the feet of 2 transit cops who wrote me a ticket.

Another time,. I learned a great deal about PROCESS. I successfully made a jump without the clerk spotting me and yelling PAY YOUR FARE through his lame speaker, but I jumped to early, and my train wasn't there yet. (Lesson 1: Time your shit so you can get right on the train and vanish),. BECAUSE the guy working the concession stand inside the platform area where you wait might DRY SNITCH on you. I watched as this little Indian cat pointed at me while speaking on the phone. Sure enough,. 2 transit cops rolled up to me and I got nervous.

"Let's see some ID" . . .

"Friday night, hmm . . . why don't we put you in holding so you can spend the weekend? . . ."

They gave me a ticket that I never paid and made me go back and pay for the ride I was trying to steal. To finish me off I got into a car with no air conditioner,. (This was the hottest week of the Summer), and the car was like 103 degrees. The only people in the car with me were a Cockroach that was getting his SAUNA on,. and another sight I'll NEVER forget, a woman with a baby carriage but instead of a baby,. she has a SMALL BULLDOG IN BABY CLOTHES in the carriage. (Was this the subway ride to a NIGHTMARE?)

This one is weak however compared to what happened to my man CB back in the 70's . . .

In the 70's the subway toilets were actually being used,. and they were a "very special place".CB was on his way to a family party, . . . and had on some sharp 70's pointed collar,bell-bottom,type clothes.He forgot his token and said, . . . Fuck it, . . . I'm jumpin this shit,. and yeah,. he got busted, . . . but its what happened next where it gets DARK.

The cop decided he was gonna teach my friend a lesson and took him into the subway bathroom.This particular bathroom was shall we say, . . . blown out . . .

He then told him to get down on his knees AND HE CUFFED HIM WITH HIS HANDS AROUND THE BOWL.

BLOWN.OUT.EYE CONTACT.

AND THEN LEFT FOR 20 MINUTES.

Then, . . . the cop came back with another jumper and cuffed HIM to the radiator pipe, . . . strung up on some prisoner shit,. and then leaves again . . .

"Nice night eh man?"

"Oh yeah,. just hanging out"

20 minutes later, . . . he freed them both, . . . and blessed them with tickets, . . . which of course got "lost".(has anybody actually payed any of those shit's?)

Needless to say,. at the party,. CB was not in the best of moods.His mom asked him where he was he said, . . ."some kind of crazy delay on the train"

2011 with Metrocards there's a whole other Hustle perspective that goes down,. especially with the unlimited cards. It's a whole other world with a lot more cops and even military on the anti-terrorism we will search your shit vibe. All I can add here is, . . .

JUST PAY YOUR SHIT.

SUBWAY DRAMA 6

As we all know,. drinking is a never ending source of drama.If your gonna be drunk past the point of being aware of who and where you are,. the subway ain't the place to be.When you fall asleep your at a higher risk to,. but being pass-out drunk is just asking for it.To bad Elliot Ness couldn't derail this crazy train that's destroyed CULTURES.Drugs to,. when you see guys on the train in nothing but their BVD's,(Tighty whiteys),. something has gone wrong,. REAL wrong.In the subway,. your world's COLLIDE.

Case in point,. the E train at West 4th around 4 am back in 1990-something.I had my trumpet with me after playing music late down in the village somewhere.There's 2 gay guys having a strange argument,. where one of them is a master and the other a slave.Nearby there's a guy sitting on the bench with his legs spread out on the verge of passing out.He's trying to sit up but having no luck.I didn't sit next to him,. just near-by.He's got a trench coat that's open with his wallet in clear view.He has a $20 bill resting on one of his legs that I keep looking at.Andrew Jackson looked pissed off.

2 woman walk by,. a little lit up,. having fun,. laughing and carrying on.They walk right by him and keep going about 20 feet when one woman stops the other.I'll never forget what she said and the way she said it:

"We should rob him . . ."

That's the kind of thing you might say as a joke,. laugh,. and then be out,. but this woman was serious,. and her objective seemed to be that she wanted to rob the drunk guy for fun.Her friend agreed and they creeped back to the man on the bench,. looking at me to see if I have anything to say.I smiled and shook my head like "Why you gotta do THAT?" (I

22

was curious about the fate of the $20 bill,. I knew he had another destination,. and thought about getting to know him better myself . . . But didn't have the cahones to step up, . . . or down rather . . .)

I wondered if the train might interrupt this weird street play,. but she never came. Bottom line is I reacted like 90% of other new yorkers,. it ain't my business, . . . plus, . . . I'm not letting my trumpet get jacked if I got involved in some shizzle. In NYC you learn to avoid shit. (the train coming could be a way out),. This was also,. straight ENTERTAINMENT.

So they creeped over and gently removed the $20 bill on his leg for an appetizer. Done. Next they peeled open his coat and ever so gently removed the wallet. He was about 15% awake, . . . and knew people where messing with him, . . . but could offer no Resistance,. other then mumbling an insult at them,. or the attempt of an insult,. since he was so out of hit. He tried to call them Bitches I think,. raising one arm about 8 inches up and giving up.

"y . . . o . . . yo . . . you . . . bi . . . da . . . ches . . . he . . ."

Mission accomplished and all they had to do was ease on down the road,. but this wasn't over yet. The hardest thing for them to do was not laugh and cause a scene or draw attention. About 20 feet away, . . . they stopped again.

"Lets get the shoes to",. I heard one of them say.

Why jack his shoes? There's something about shoes that goes beyond when it comes to this kind of shit. I think mostly they wanted to jack his foot machines for FUN. They got this far,. why not finish this cat off . . .

Sure enough,. they came back,. and slowly and carefully,. peeled off one shoe at a time,. like shoe retail pros from Florsheim and shit,. with those old foot measuring things. They worked as a team,. one woman gently holding his leg up ready to SSHH him if he started to wake up. Once they got the shoes they left the station for good. (I could hear them start laughing going up the stairs). They left homeboy with no money and no shoes,. complete with one skunked up toe jetting out from his ratty socks.

The train finally came through, . . . and suddenly the drunk guy was WIDE awake, . . . but couldn't understand why he had no shoes. He started looking for them,. asking me, . . . "Have you seen my shoes?"

Right before I got on the train, . . . I told him . . . "You got jacked man."

Reminds me of that one night I was driving a dodge caravan upstate and parked it one night near the bridge in Poughkeepsie,. with all my clothes in the back seat.

I'll never forget this guy that came up to me the next morning WEARING MY PANTS,. and said,.

"Man, . . . I think somebody busted into your ride man."

"Is that so?"

SUBWAY DRAMA 7

One day I just barley make it on the 7 train,. and get a seat in the end of the car where they have 2 seat benches. As the doors close a kid around 15 forces himself in and sits right down next to me and tries to act cool as soon as he sits down. There's not enough room,. whatever I'll deal with it.

The train doesn't pull out however . . .

Suddenly the doors reopen and 2 men rush in one of them with a GUN out,. and they grab up the kid next to me,. who is trying to get into his backpack. They choke hold him and take his bag.

"Is this what you wanted to get!?",. the one undercover transit police cop said,. as he PULLED A PISTOL OUT THE BAG . . .

As they pulled this KID out the train,. service was restored,. and I was left to my thoughts.

HOLY.SHIT.

Sometimes it gets violent down there,. sometimes the shit just gets out of control. Twice,. I've seen woman getting harassed with 2 different endings . . .

The first time a whole gang of teenagers come into a car looking for trouble,. (remember Bernard Goetz,. the subway vigilante?) . . . They didn't want to rob anyone,. but rather make this one woman VERY uncomfortable,. by getting over the Top SEXUAL with her, . . . like a gang rape vibe without actually doing it. One guy near me tries to stop them, . . .

"Come on guys,. this isn't cool,. leave her alone . . ."

The leader of the pack: "WHATCHU GONNA DO LITTLE MAN?!"

"YOU KNOW,. U GOT A FACE THAT SURE LOOKS PUNCHABLE. THE KIND OF FACE I JUST WANT TO PUNCH."

Suddenly,. a big African looking guy in a big trench coat grabs the leader of the pack and puts him up on the bars that we hold onto when we have to stand. His undercover badge is hanging out,. transit cop,. undercover . . .

COP: "YOU WANT TO GO TO JAIL TONIGHT??!! CAUSE THAT SHIT CAN BE ARRANGED!!"

(Sweet! This was getting interesting,. he has to back down right?)

Wrong,. that MACHO shit has him fighting back. FUCK YOU. LET ME GO . . . His crew knows the deal and forces him to cool out. They HELP the cop subdue him and tell him to cool the Fuck out. Next stop the kids force there friend of the train and the cop follows calling for backup. As we pull out I look at the woman they were messing with,. and she was relieved, . . . Shook,. but relieved . . .

That Macho shit is so ridiculous. I had a friend who had to do more time in Jail because he wouldn't apologise to a judge.

Worse is another situation where you see violent parents hitting and screaming on their kids,. I HATE being up in that shit. A few times I've been around it,. and just wait to get the hell off the train. Sometimes it's not up to the cops to handle shit,. and the public steps in.I've seen a different form of justice on the train.BRUTAL justice,. at least to me.As usual in this next one,. somebody has had TO MUCH to drink . . .

7 train.Daytime.Going to Manhattan between Roosevelt ave and Queens plaza,end of the car in the small seats.A woman is sitting down,minding her own business,with a drunk guy sitting across from her with a twisted smile.A JOKER wanna be.The drunk guy decides that insulting the woman would be fun.

"You ugly Bitch.".

He starts laughing, . . . he thinks this is great.

"You Skanky HOE"

The woman is clearly uncomfortable, . . . but not fighting back, . . . she stays quiet.

Homeboy keeps it up,. and now some of us are getting Tight.I myself am ready to step in, . . . but it wont be necessary,. not today.

This HUGE guy, . . . and his girl come over, . . . TIGHT.

The big guy gets in the drunks face.

"I'M GONNA SAY THIS BUT ONE TIME.YOUR GONNA SIT THERE AND SHUT UP.ONE MORE WORD OUT OF YOU AND YOUR GONNA ANSWER, . . . TO ME."

The drunk guy is shocked, . . . and he stays quiet for about one minute.The huge guy is half-watching, . . . thinking he squashed it.

"You ugly bitch . . ." he's says to the woman . . .

In a blink of an eye, . . . the huge guy was back, . . . and he was NOT playing.

"WHAT THE HELL DID I TELL YOU?!?!. NOW YOUR GONNA LEARN A DIFFICULT LESSON".

He forces the guy up out of the chair and POW! hits him right in the face. POW! One more once. The drunk guy is clearly hurt. The huge guy puts him back in his seat, . . . and then HIS GIRL gets in the drunk guys face.

"You piece of shit. He told you to stay quiet. Look at you now. LOOK AT YOU NOW."

Drunk guy starts openly crying, . like a child and shit.

The whole time, . . . the woman being insulted said nothing, and spoke to no-one. She quietly got off after another couple of stops. After she left, . the huge guy and his girl left, . . . leaving me with the drunk guy.

He started crying again, . . . and looked at me the same way a 5 year old does when his toy car breaks.

What could I say?

As I left the car, . . . I said "You got served man, . turn it down with the damn Crazy Horse, . and maybe you'll see better" . . .

Have to wonder what's happening right. now. Wonder if that guy is even still alive.

SUBWAY DRAMA 8

Not all the subway drama is life or death,. although they may seem that way.Sometimes there just STUPID.

Queens plaza,. underground.A hub connecting all of the Queens trains and Manhattan. Above ground,. a pretty depressed area.

To "see" this one, . . . you have to see that at Queens plaza,. express and local trains run side by side for periods of time, . . . and between stations you can see right into the car across from you until the local stops, . . . and the express eases on down the road. (towards Roosevelt ave Jackson heights where I lived for 6 years.THE most DIVERSE area on Earth).

Standing on the platform one day,one guy decides to straight throw his trash on the ground, . . . looked like food he didn't want.Another man standing near him took what he did personally and straight commanded the trash guy, . . . to "PICK UP YOUR TRASH".The other guy couldn't believe he was being stepped to and said, . . .

"You pick it up asshole!.".

A nice FUCK YOU!,. then brought these 2 actually towards a physical confrontation over TRASH,. for talking trash!

Thankfully a train showed up and the trash throwing guy got on,. still talking TRASH, . . . and making threats.Stupidly, . . . I got in the same car,. which took off, . . . drama over right?

NAH ...

The next train across the platform from us pulls up RIGHT next to in transit,as I explained before ... and the car with the guy who got pissed off about the other guy dropping trash is in the car RIGHT across from us.The other guy in my car sees him, ... and they both go to the same opposing windows and continue making counter threats through the glass, ... of which they each can barely hear!

The guy in my car is screaming, ... "ROOSEVELT!" ... stating that that's the stop where they can meet and finish off this drama for real, ... and of course Roosevelt is my stop. You could tell the other guy understood "Roosevelt",. and intended to meet us there.The trains stopped being in sync and off to Roosevelt we went.

Once there, ... I broke out, ... not waiting to see how it played out, ... but as I was going up the stairs I heard a woman scream, ... and I couldn't help but take a quick look,. rubbernecking.

The guy I was with waited for the local train,. and the other guy chose to come to Roosevelt to continue this ridiculous shit.Now, ... both on the platform again, ... these 2 guys were now in a full on fight,pushing and slapping,. a weird looking fight.

Nearby is a DIANETICS STRESS TEST TABLE,. where people try to convince you that you need to learn Dianetics to save your life,. or at least,. that you need to buy a book and keep them going.I took the test in Boston,. and they told me that I was SUICIDAL,. and that Dianetics was the only way out,. before they sat me down with a video by Chick Corea,. a great jazz pianist.(I declined)

So when the 2 GARBAGE MEN came and DESTROYED THE WHOLE TABLE with their fight,. I had to smile and laugh,.

Man,. they were grabbing each others coats and fell right in the CENTER of the tables,. sending the machines, books, posters, and 2 administrators right to the floor . . . Is this what the whole thing was really about?

Seeing Dianetics go down hard like that made my day,. and brings a smile even now.

Revenge comes,. in MANY forms. It reminds of a WEED related story. See me on the personal for that . . . not enough weed stories for a book.

SUBWAY DRAMA 9

Something about going DOWN,. underground . . . when you enter the Subway. It seems there is an actual decent of the human condition. The standards by what we live by above ground seem to get, . . . compromised. In the end,. human beings are souls in bodies,. and we have always been at the mercy of them. The rest room is a part of our culture,. and when you enter the Subway,. you no longer have access to what is a vital part of our lives. Life gets real when something so simple is placed out of reach. Just. Have. To. Get. HOME . . . or the nearest Starbucks. I almost got into a fight at a Starbucks once when somebody tried to FORCE their way into the bathroom I was using. There's so many examples of this,. but I don't think you can find one person in NYC who hasn't faced this drama at least once . . . How simple and fragile we can be . . .

The R train goes underground from Queens to NYC,. and was the site of my earliest subway drama . . . I'm headed home one day after work,. pretty crowded car and I'm in a car that has both ends locked. People change cars all the time this way,. and usually the doors are open,. but not in this car. While we are right in the middle between the city and the borough,. the train stops,. and the power gets shut down,. although we still have light. No explanation,. (The R has the worst intercom of the line anyway) . . .

That's when I notice a woman standing near me that actually appears to have a green face. She is not well. People near her are looking at her like,. "wow,. she looks horrible",. but what can any of us do? She's at WAR with her body,. and is about to lose, . . .

Bad . . .

Yes,. as in my Q33 Bus drama later on,. she was the sick passenger that the Train is always telling in their broken announcements,. "If your sick,. do NOT get on board." Yes,. to her own Horror,. her body forces her to THROW UP. BIG TIME.

The whole car shifted with about 40 people actually trying to shift away from her,. in a panic vibe. If we were on a mountaintop,. we would have shifted the weight all the way,. and crashed to our doom. If we were on a boat we would have capsized. The doors are LOCKED,. as some people are like,. "Oh hell no,. I'm changing cars!" . . .

I really felt bad for her,. but could not help seeing a full GRAPE 2 inches from my sneaker . . . shit . . . did you have to swallow that shit WHOLE girl?

She clearly feels way better,. but is now embarrassed beyond belief,. for a woman imparticular,. I know this was traumatizing.

Worse,. is what happens next,. as a guy starts HITTING ON HER.

WHAT?

"Wow,. I can see you feel a lot better . . . wish there was something I could do,. (really?!),. in fact,. here's my card and my number,. I would love to get together sometime. Can I call you? Get your number?" The woman didn't get angry,. she smiled and made eye contact,. maybe he was doing this to help her vibe. A true playa can stand in someones vomit and make the move like it ain't no thang,. after all right? A group of us looked at each other like,. WTF?.

The train,. with no power,. had no air,. and we were stuck there for 40 minutes. Let's just say that car started to KICK with a special vibe . . .

*   *   *

Next drama,. and last of this kind thank God,. happened to a good friend of mine,. let's call him RALPH. This is NASTY,. but my favorite. This my friends,. is a story about SURVIVAL . . .

So late one night,. my man Ralph is on the platform really late,. with nobody around . . . His body is FREAKING out,. and DEMANDING that he DROP NUMBER 2,. or shall we say have an EXTREME BOWEL MOVEMENT RIGHT AWAY . . . Many of us have experienced this,. but sometimes,. the body just doesn't take NO for an answer. You might think you have this under control, . . . maybe . . . For my man Ralph,. It reaches the point where he just as no choice.

"Shit!!, . . . is anybody around?"

With no one there to be a problem,. Ralph drops it like it's HOT right on the platform . . . then,. a true survivor,. Ralph uses his pocket knife to cut off his underwear and clean himself,. placing the underwear on top of his victory pile,. like a sheet over a dead body or something . . .

His timing is perfect as the train arrives and no one has seen him.

His gift to the MTA left for the world to enjoy . . .

Damn,. that's some wild shit . . . and sometimes we just do what we gotta do . . .

TAKE THAT YOU CORRUPT MTA BASTARDS.

SUBWAY DRAMA 10

When you face perpetual lack of sleep,. you learn strategy in NYC . . . With SUMMER INSOMNIA Haunting me,. I would always tell myself late at night staring at the clock,. "It's OK,. I can always sleep on the 7".

If I got to the 7 and got one of the "edge" seats,. where I only have to sit next to one person,. and can lean my head back,. I might be able to get 20-30 minutes of SLEEP. When I was really tired,. I would plan this and try to make it happen. When your that tired,. 20 minutes can really help,. at least for me,. for others that makes it worse.

What I did was actually not cool. Entering at times a DEEP sleep,. I was especially vulnerable,. and sometimes I was with my entire family of horns,. that I tried to place under or near me in a way,. that if somebody tried to take one,. it would wake me up. Sometimes I wanted to stay awake,. and my body would just SHUT ME DOWN . . . Having a bad case of SLEEP APNEA didn't help,. I've been to sleep disorder clinics twice,. the whole drama,. with electrodes on your dome and cameras in the ceiling. I've had friends get robbed while they where asleep,. one friend had his wallet in his front shirt pocket and when he woke up,. somebody cut the bottom of the pocket with a knife,and took it while he slept. Luckily,. I was never picked like this myself, . . . BUT,.

I did wake up with my head on the shoulder of a little Asian dude,. who got pissed . . .

I also woke up with my hand on some dude's leg.(I woke up by another person picking my arm up and putting it back on my lap.)

I'll also never forget 2 short Mexican guys,. twins!,. wearing full TEX MEX gear,. that were asleep leaning on each other,. and when the train shifted,. they shifted together,. poetry in motion . . .

And as the Sun starts to set . . . (It's getting a little dark in here)

I fell asleep and missed my stop on the 1/9 train and ended up in Harlem during Rush hour, . . . and got woke up because a guy was really pissed and yelling at a guy across from us to STOP JERKING OFF ON THE TRAIN.

"IT'S WAY TO EARLY FOR THIS SHIT MAN!"

A friend of mine on a COCAINE binge woke up on the FLOOR of the F train,. 5 hours after he got on.(He had run the whole route twice).People walked over him like he wasn't even there.

And for the last, . . . 7 train pulls in to NYC,. and a guy is full on stretched out on a bench,. asleep like he was at home and shit.He was GONE,. taking up the whole seat.The train emptied out but this guy didn't even know where he was.

The conductor comes out,. like a 6 foot 5 inch guy with the big headphones and all the MTA gear,. and he sees this guy SNORING all loud.

I decide to stick around and enjoy the show . . .

"Last stop.", . . . the conductor says, . . . (no response)

"LAST.STOP." . . . the conductor says,. right in homeboys ear, . . . (still no response)

So the conductor ROLLS HIM OFF THE BENCH TO HIT THE FLOOR . . .

BAMN!

DAMN, . . . what a way to wake up, . . . shit . . .

The sleep guy is awake now, . and wants to fight, . but cant even stand, . so he hobbles of the train pissed and disoriented.

Conductor smirks and heads back to work, . . .

"Idiot", . he says under his breath as he walks away and I head up to work . . .

"Wait!, . . . did I leave my shit on the train?!"

SUBWAY DRAMA 11

The Subway and the mentally ill have always shared a special connection. Add booze, drugs, or both to the situation and it can go NOVA.

Just today a disgruntled boyfriend went on a killing rampage that ended in the 3 train at Times Square. It ended when he attacked a man with 3 kids,. brandishing a huge bloody knife,. I just saw the story on the news.

"Your going to Die!",. the attacker said.

Family guy fought back and survived,. before the cops took out the Maniac.

Just a few days earlier I took a chance at presenting a man with the chance for redemption vs him attacking me,. and there's no telling if he was carrying a weapon:

The A train uptown,. packed,. rush hour,. and here comes ANGRY DRUNK RACISM guy.

This cat was African American and PISSED . . .

One by one he went to each person on the train and dressed them down for their heritage or whatever beef he could find. No one was sparred,. meaning African Americans were also targeted for selling out or being slaves to the man.

Everybody was scared but trying to ignore it,. and then he ramped it up and crossed the line:

He got in an old woman's face,. (also black),. and demanded money.

"I'M NOT GOOD ENOUGH TO BREAK OFF SOME CHANGE?!!?"

The elder lady whispered,almost crying,. "I'm so tired and just want to go home" . . .

I'm not sure what happened next,. but as I was thinking . . . "Am I supposed to help this guy?",I found myself with him,. making me the next target and he "released" the old woman.

He started by smacking my Spider-man comic book out my hand to the floor.I can take that.He then demanded an explanation of what I was reading represented.

This soon went to a supreme test of my emotional intelligence when he tried to egg me into a fight.I wasn't buying.When I didn't fight he oddly started unburdening himself to me like we were in a confessional.He admitted that if he wasn't drunk,. he was a real person . . . Ive heard that shit before.

Me:"You want to end up like my friend Giuseppi?"

Man:"WhO ThE FuCk iS ThAt?!"

Me:My boy G has 12 kids but no family.He's 76 with nothing and still chasing drugs.He has destroyed his life.

Man:"WHaTs FamIlY gOT tO WiTh tHiS ShIt?"

Me:"Don't you see that bag your holding IS your FAMILY?"

Man:"How DARE you?!!? RrRrRrrrrrRRRRRRRRRRRRRRRRRRRRraaahhhhahahahah!!!

I knew I crossed the line when he lost it and I got ready to fight, . . . when he slumped down in the seat and spoke soberly and quietly.

Man: "I know your right . . . I'm no addict though,. I could stop" . . .

As the train stopped he unexpectedly bounced,. had I CUT him to close?

Man: "Thank you sir"

STREET PRIEST HAD STRUCK AGAIN.

All my life I have been led to help people in unexpected and unusual ways in unexpected and unusual places,. it's part of my life.

SUBWAY DRAMA 12

Been a rough couple days down in the NYC trenches . . .

Living uptown in Washington Heights at 163rd and Broadway I have some new trains to get into. The *D* has stolen the show.

DOWNTOWN to work this morning back at Sam Ash,. a whole other world of drama's.

When I get on the packed rush hour to work train I'm trying to listen to the mix of my new CD on my IPOD.

Not today . . .

The LOUDEST preacher I have ever heard on the subway has this car on LOCKDOWN.

The WHOLE car looks like their in pain. I just cant concentrate or listen to anything without this guy spreading his infection.

JESUS.JESUS.JESUS.JESUS.JESUS.JESUS.JESUS.JESUS.JESUS.JESUS.JESUS.JESUS.JESUS.JESUS.

Look,. If that's what somebody needs to validate their life,. so be it . . . but I'm all ready TAXED going to work,. and this cat is relentless and ruthless,. just not giving up. He was in the ZONE when I got on,. and then stayed in it all the way downtown. I found the ability some people had to ignore him amazing,. especially those sitting close to him. Some people made fun of him. Most important,. as I noticed so many times before,. He reached NOBODY. These people have a compulsion to save and defeat Satan,. but no one is listening,. just further validating their war on SATAN.For the first half of my trip I was SO close to screaming "WILL YOU JUST SHUT THE *** UP!!!",. But what's the point? I would become Satan myself at this point,. and I'm working on not taking shit personal,. like stupid shit at work.NYC wears on the mind.

UPTOWN,. Going home from work

The D is less crowded and I'm trying to chill,. I got music on my mind.

A woman walks right up to me and stops and explains in a horrible stutter that she is the victim of experimental drugs!

"WHAT?" She actually did that shit?! She's saying it's the truth,and hard for her to busk for change.She is truly hurting and can hardly walk or talk over this.Doing the experimental drug routine is something some people do desperate for cash,. but . . .

DAMN.

Worse,. a 5 year old kid from the other side keeps interrupting her,.

"Want to bring your speech over here?"

I thought he and his family had money for her,. but they just brought her over to make fun of her!

I gave her $5,. more than I ever give . . . and thought of the guy with no legs dragging himself through,. and all the other people with destroyed lives that live down there.

Closer to home,. the hip hop Beat boy dance crew enters the car and sets up there beat box for their improv give us change routine.

"Were out here to stay out of trouble,. earn money for uniforms,. blah blah . . ."

Damn flips almost knocked my glasses off.(heh)

Well,. there you have it folks . . .

This closes my special chapter on Life in the NYC subway. I hope you enjoyed the ride. Please feel free to come on through anytime,. day or night . . .

I'll dedicate this first part of the book to:

All the people that sell the STREET NEWS,. and offer food for the homeless . . . I read a great article in SN once by a fellow musician. A bona fide paper.

The DEAF folks that come in and put SIGN LANGUAGE CARDS on everybody's leg,. asleep or not,. and then go around and collect if no one buys or offers a donation. It's rare that anyone does.

The folks with NO LEGS,. moving through the center looking for change

ALL the loco PREACHERS AND BEGGARS

The DANCERS, TEX MEX MUSICIANS, COMEDIANS, ALL DRUMMERS, MUSICIANS, AND ARTISTS, . . . especially my man,. LOVE SUPREME,. a sax player . . . and also,. those BUCKET, PAIL, AND PAN DRUMMERS . . .

ALL OF US WENT THROUGH 9/11, . . . THE BLACKOUT,. AND THE TRANSIT STRIKE TOGETHER . . .

I'll close with my friend,. Crazy exploding briefcase guy: . . .

I'm inside the I train and the doors are closing . . .

BAM!

Some wall street,. lawyer guy throws his briefcase between the doors to force them open and force himself on the train.

Translation: "I don't give a fuck about the train or anybody on it,. I'm going to HOLD this shit up,. even risking my shit . . . I am one DESPERATE and stupid MO FO."

Bad move man . . .

The conductor doesn't see the guy,. and he's already started pulling out, . . . with the guys briefcase stuck between the doors . . .

Homeboy starts running with us,. PULLING AND SCREAMING, . . .

"STOP THE TRAIN, . . . MY BRIEFCASE! AHHHHHH!"

I'm right inside the door and figure, . . . "well,. he DID ask for my help . . ."

So I BOOT THAT SHIT out of the doors . . .

The briefcase EXPLODES . . .

CONTRACTS IN THE WIND . . .

I tried to go through the doors between the cars and throw him something that fell out inside the car,. but it was to late . . . we were in the Tunnel.

Crazy exploding briefcase guy was left to ask himself some serious questions,.

About LIFE . . .

ALL.ABOARD.

Now lets go take a ride on the BUS. We have a long way to go before we get home.

BUS DRAMA 1

The Q32 BUS goes from Jackson Heights to the city and back,. by way of the 59th st bridge.Always late,always PACKED.I remember it most for this guy I saw all the time with Turrets syndrome,. always cursing us all out.The Bus is not immune from the drama series,. not by a long shot.

This one particular day,. were headed all the way,. to round one at least . . .

BUS DRIVER VS CRAZY QUEENS GUY

DING.DING

I get on one day,. late evening,. and I'm in the middle of the bus,. which was moving. Late evening was less traffic,less people.Some guy is sitting up front (In THIS corner we have . . .) . . . and he's got an issue with the driver that I don't know about.This particular street guy(not the turrets guy I just mentioned) is sitting there making threats to the driver.KICK YOUR ASS!, . . . comes out loud through some street gibberish.He's rocking back and forth,. left to right.(never a good sign).There's some weird Racial shit going down to,. although both the driver and the street guy are minorities.

(And in THIS corner),. The driver,. is trying to keep his cool, . . . and says,. "Sir, . . . you need to be quiet,. and not interfere with the driver,. especially with the bus in motion".Were going about 20-30 mph.I'm watching this shit thinking if I should act.

Crazy,pissed off guy,. decides hes gonna take it to the next level,. and while where in motion, . . . tries to get in the drivers face and make this shit personal.His coat,. in the summertime,. is WAY to big,. and he gets right up in the drivers space past the bar that separates him,. waving his arms and talking weird shit,. oblivious that were moving,. or doesn't care if we crash.Somebody needs to step up, . . . that is unless the driver can,.

S'ok, . . . He GOT THIS.

With one hand on the wheel,the driver forces the guy back with his other hand,. "SIR!!,. WHAT THA?!,.YOU CANT, . . . SIT THE FUCK DOWN!".

Bus swerves a little,. but the driver is still in control . . . Unfortunately,. the crazy guy needs more, . . . attention,. and returns to the drivers space,. more aggressive and loud than before . . . We veer off again,. not really slowing down,. and now everybody is scared as shit.

So the Driver decides to HANDLE SHIT . . .

With his left hand on the wheel,. he gets up,. and COLD COCKS the crazy guy in the face,. sending him backward into his seat,. KNOCKED OUT.(Sugar Ray Leonard would be proud).The crazy guy is slumped over,. like he was asleep.

1, . . . 2!, . . . 3!, . . .

The Driver regained control of the bus, . . . and started trying to pull over to throw homeboy out . . .

"I TOLD YOU TO STEP THE FUCK OFF.SEE WHAT HAPPENS? KNOCK YOUR ASS OUT AGAIN."

We pulled over,. and he woke crazy guy up,. and threw him of the bus . . . Outside,. the crazy guy goes,. "Drive away!,. Drive away!,.

"GET IN FRONT FIRST"., driver says as we pull out.

BUS DRIVER: 1

CRAZY GUY: 0

As we resumed the route, . . . a limp, sporadic applause leaked out. The driver was yelling to himself.

"MESS WITH ME? PAY THE PRICE! YOU PAY TO PLAY WITH ME!"

I got off soon after that, . . . holding on to my bass-clarinet extra tight, . . . like when you don't want a little kid to cross the street.

Gotta give the driver PROPS. We were all in danger, . . . but he luckily squashed it the best way he could in the moment. We were lucky we didn't all get Hurt,. bad.

Before I leave though,. the whole Bus trips on a woman outside wearing clothes WAY to small for her 300 pound plus frame,. almost like she was a stripper. As we pass her,. several woman cry out,. OH MY GAWD, . . . NO SHE DIDN'T . . .

On my way to the subway transfer to the city . . . hope those Hip Hop teenage PIMPS don't harass me again and make me late . . .

BUS DRAMA 2

The Q33 Bus goes from Laguardia airport to Jackson Heights in Queens and back. That's it. It loops and loops,. almost always packed. I remember it most for not stopping at my stop on the brickest (coldest) days of the year,. because there was no more room,. or the driver wasn't feeling my vibe ...

I got on at Roosevelt ave,(Yes,. Roosevelt again),near little India,and was going home one day. By the census,. Jackson Heights is the most diverse barrio in the WHOLE COUNTRY. Korea,Panama,Columbia,Mexico,India,and even Afghanistan and Israel on the same block. There's some loco Trans gender club near my stop to top it all off. The first thing I noticed on the bus this particular day was this "Wall street" guy, ... sitting near the front. Immaculate suit,. briefcase, . . . and most notably,. uncomfortable,. out of his environment. The Q33 was 98% not white,. and not for people loaded with cash. The bus was filling to the max. Almost nobody spoke English,. adding to wall street guy's vulnerability. This guy should have just taken a cab,I thought. doesn't look like $ is a problem for him.

So halfway to the airport,. moving slow in traffic,. (hope you don't need to get there fast man.),the bus driver lets on this street guy in a tore up black trench coat with a crazy red beard. This guy has a huge beer can barley being covered by a tore up brown bag. He's spilling shit,. got the shakes,and is stinking up the bus,. DRUNK. Bus drivers call,. after awhile they don't care or try to control this shit,. it's every man for himself.(Hey,. maybe red beard worked on wall street for a minute,. see where it can lead?)

Beer guy forces himself through,. right near WALL street guy,. and stands right on top of him. Wall street is sitting down in a tight cramped 3 seater. Wall street guy is starting to feel the pressure,. I can see him agitated and nervous,. stressed out.(Didn't his company pay for a massage or something?).My "street alarm" went off and told me to back away,. I was right next to both of these freaks.I pushed myself uncomfortably into a little old Spanish woman,. who had no reaction at all.(You learn to turn yourself off in these places)

Beer guy: . . . "Uh-oh, . . . I don't feel so good" . . . (he was genuinely upset)

You know what happened next . . .

Beer guy HURLS ALL OVER WALL STREET . . .

SUIT.BRIEFCASE,. the whole 9 . . .

. . . .

Wall street guy FREAKS.

AhHhHhHhHhHhHh! WHAT THE HELL IS WRONG WITH YOU?!

I'M ON MY WAY TO CATCH A PLANE!!!!!!!

. . . .

Bus pulls over.It's been TWO stops.

Beer guy: "I'm sorry, . . . but BOY, . . . do I FEEL better!!".(gets off)

I got off 2 stops after that,. with maybe a little HURL on my shoe.Nobody said shit to wall street.Not the driver,nor any passengers offered him any help.The look on his face said it all.I'll never forget what these 2 old ladies said that got off the Bus with me,.

"I feel like I just got beaten up . . ."

The fate of wall street guy remains unknown,. but I wont front,. I didn't feel to bad for him.

If only it could have been Mike DOOMberg . . . I mean GLOOMberg, . . . or,.

..Um..yeah.. . . .

POST OFFICE DRAMA 1

Aside from the SUBWAY and BUS dramas in NYC,. the Post office is also a special place,. where the public can spend quality time together,. Kind of like the DMV express near Madison square Garden. The Post Office is the site for 2 of my NYC stories . . . more to come I'm sure. I haven't been in a DMV in years,. I take the Subway.

This was the post office near my day gig at Tower records,. and I was there frequently. Although they have a sign of their customer service supervisor framed on the wall,. (next to BUSH at the time),. I never saw this person. The MTA has these pictures to,. with phone numbers that lead to nowhere.(They should a picture of a rat,. There the one's running shit.) At the PO,. there are never enough clerks,. and always a line,. sometimes a 45 minute plus line,. and in NYC,. we don't have time for that shit.(Just Like back in the 70's,. when we waited 2 hours online for GAS,. and then the guy came and put a big sign on the car in front of us,. NO MORE GAS) The PO staff is never around when you need them,a DIVERSE group as always,. at least we have that worked out,. (or do we?) Spending so much time on line,. you end up seeing that the place is just not run right,. much like the GOVERNMENT itself,. a runaway train that no-one can stop. It can get THICK in NYC when people try to RISE up on line . . . any line really . . .

Here's what went down in front of me in PO DRAMA 1

A LONG, TIRED LINE,. about 40-60 people,. but only 2 clerks,. mid-day,. Columbus and 67th,. (lots of happy staff in the back though).All we can hear is broken,confused,conversation at the windows(torture to me),. somebodies earphones,. a buzzer that wont stop,. and this, . . .

This ONE guy,.

Taking the art of being the cell phone asshole to the level known as NEXT . . .

. . . .

REALLY loud,. with the whole office hearing his stupid shit, . . . blah,. blah,. blah, . . . I'm right near this crackpipe . . .

The guy right behind him is really getting tired of it,. like a man in a cage,. (like all of us?)

Course, . . . hes not gonna do something about it, . . . right?

WRONG.

Like some HOLLYWOOD shit.

The guy behind him GRABS the phone OUT of the guys hand and ENDS the call.

"Your disconnected, . . ." (He said it fairly calm, . . . the WHOLE place stopped and watched).

"WHAT the hell?

The guy who was talking didn't know what the hell happened . . . he couldn't fathom that his call was over and that this guy had his phone. This is something that we JUST DON'T DO. He decided the phone was the issue,. getting it back. The guy that took it said nothing,. but looked unstable.

"Give me my phone back."

GIVE ME MY PHONE.

The guy tries to get his phone,. and the other guy winds up, . . . steps back and

HURLS THAT SHIT to the floor, . . . breaking it into pieces.One part slid over and bounced off my foot! (maybe you can see the slow-motion shattering,. parts flying,shocked expressions,and my smile)

AAAHHHH! The whole PO and seemingly the WORLD was at a DEAD STOP,. (like the Subway and Bus LOVE to do) . . .

The guy who got cut off was MAD, . . . and also SCARED.He decided the best option was to just LEAVE.

After he stormed out, . . . a few people went over to the CELL PHONE SMASHER.One reached out and shook this hand . . . "OK man?"

"Nice work" . . .

(A little guilty, . . . but seemingly satisfied)

"Thanks" . . .

I helped the janitor cat pick up a few celly pieces,and we looked at each at the same time. We didn't say it out loud,. but could hear each other's thoughts,.

"Damn!,. that was some shit to see."

In mere seconds,. I'm Back on line,.

The NYC MACHINE cHuRnS on . . .

POST OFFICE DRAMA 2

$ FREE.MONEY.$

Just about everybody has been walking on the street and seen money just laying there in the SUN saying, . . . "Hi!, . . . pick my ass up!!" . . . $. When your a kid, . . . its a whole different ball game,. because money's not rent and food, . . . its just, . . . MONEY, . . . so I'm still cool with those 40 beans I found in the bathroom at Yankee stadium in 1978.(I can still name the whole team.) In NYC,. it happens more often,. of course,. with millions of us on a mission of some kind to rule the world.

As a rule most people that I've discussed "found money" with say,. if you see the person drop the money,. or you know who the money belongs to,. you have to return it to them . . . (still, . . . temptation comes.).If you found a wallet,. there's more of a switch-up, . . . some people say they would call or mail it or whatever,. but SOME people say, . . . "I'm taking the money,. and then sending the wallet", . . . or,. "fuck it, . . . that shit is mine now.$

I've never found a wallet, . . . but I HAVE lost one and had it returned to me, . . . complete with the 3 dollars inside.(this drama don't mean much when you are sometimes broke as hell like my ass.).Still,. back in the day we didn't have all the important shit that we carry around with us like we do now.NEVER leave shit in a cab.(A good friend of mine lost a mini-disc,a bass wheel,and a bass amp) The Taxi Lost and found is a JOKE.When I was a messenger I left A BAG OF CHECKS on the bus, . . . and somebody turned then in! (An older woman I was told,. a guardian angel?).

I can recall vividly the times Ive been in the free money situation. Finding a woman's purse with nothing in it in jersey city, . . . and back, BACK in the day when I was cleaning movie theatres between shows, . complete with an ORANGE JUMPSUIT.

Back in the locker room, . . . this cat Cyrus had a wallet and was counting, . . .

20, . 40, . 60, . . . $

"What you got there man?"

"What?, . man you better get hip, . . . wallets fall out of pockets and people leave not knowing, . there to into the movies, . . . first thing you do is not clean, . you go up and down and see if somebody needs to get jacked." $

The wallet Cyrus had was PACKED with shit, . He peeled me off a $20 to keep me cool, teach me something, . and buy me lunch. $

The time FREE MONEY really had me on the ropes was the same PO from POST OFFICE DRAMA ONE.

I'm on a lunch break from my job around the corner and I look down over where you drop off mail inside, . and there's a PILE OF CASH sitting there on the floor . . . Looks like BENJAMIN'S and JACKSON'S. (Fuck Wash and Link, . they ain't got shit to say) $

. . . .

OK, . . . who owns this shit?, . . . nobodies even seeing this but me? This is a public office, . they have RULES and shit. Maybe somebody will come back. $

Nobodies coming back.If I turn this in to the post office, . . . what will they do?,. There's no way to PROVE this belongs to anybody. If the person who LOST it figures out they LOST it,. how would they know where to LOOK? If I'm gonna do something,. it better be quick!

Isn't there a CAMERA on me RIGHT now? What if I "get caught"?,. JAIL IS NOT FOR ME.(Thanks SCARED STRAIGHT,. I could have had a job selling WEED and ACID door to door with a pager once) $

Fuck it, . . . I'm taking this shit, . . . Ill figure it out later.

I took the money and tried to stay cool,. leaving immediately even though I had business to take care off mailing shit . . .

Outside,. a guy in biker shorts comes up to me.(I'm walking away quickly,. about 50 feet,. and haven't even counted the $ yet)

"I saw you take that money.I want some".

Now THIS was out, . . . more out than the actual drama, . . . this guy had some rationale that he had a right to it just like me because it wasn't mine.I guess it was the people's money now.He was a white dude in biker shorts in case any body is trying to drop a stereotype.

Hmm, . . . I'll bet 20$ will cool your ass out.$ (It did) . . .

Back at my job,. I had a real morality CRISIS,. from listening to so much TRANE I think, . . . I'm always trying to BE A BETTER PERSON.I had to make this shit right, . . . to me.I sought street council from my boy CB who thought I was insane for having any issue at all.Man,. CB had a ball with me having the issue.

I was the head of the shipping and receiving crew at the time, . . . so I called my crew together, . . . like 6 people,. and PEELED them each off a CRISP 20$. This was win,. win, . . . I felt better, . . . and so did my crew, . . . (I cat was broke.) . . . I gave CB $60 for street council.$

Then the kicker, . . . the money I had left was THE EXACT MONEY I OWED A GOOD FRIEND. So, . . . my debt was paid.$

So what happened? Karma?

I don't know, . . . twas some crazy shit. I feel it WAS Karma,. and a TEST . . .

Did I Pass?

Don't know.

What would you do?, . . .

Here's your chance to confess.

Get it off your chest.

Come on, . . .

What, . . . have you DONE?

. . . .

As the title of my first book of at least 3 suggests,here is the section BEYOND the NYC trenches.Some of it happens in NYC,and some does not.It's very much a continued walk through humanity up and close.At least from an American perspective in 2011.I am still the eyes in all these real life scenarios.I'm sure there are deeper and deeper levels of humanity in places like Japan who just had a major Tidal Wave.Haiti,. from their Earthquake,and of course,beyond.

As a musician I spent December of last year playing Christmas tunes in the subway on my flugelhorn.Some people said,. "Bless you",as they dropped me a dollar.One person left a Big Mac wrapper in my case.I met a friend from Africa.

One day I was followed around by a guy with a big sign that said JUDGEMENT DAY MAY 21ST 2011.Whenever I moved this guy followed me making me part of delivering his message,driving me nuts.I finally asked him how he knew it was the end and he told me it was the 31,000 year anniversary of the flood from the Bible,. the one from Noah's ark when the whole world was flooded.I said really? He said with complete assurance,absolutely no doubt,that time was up.

If your reading this,we survived.The great 2012 comes next.

Will we make it BEYOND 2012? As a friend says,. will the human race make it out of our protracted adolescence?

NYC BEYOND DRAMA 1

BIKE JACK

Never get to comfortable in NYC . . .

As long as Ive been up in this mess,. and I've been HUSTLED at least twice by, . . . "professionals", . . . (my 3 card Monte event was an initiation like no other) . . . you can still get PICKED. Anytime, Anyplace . . . (no,. I don't mean anything like the Janet Jackson song).

It's the west side highway bike path last week or so,. and I'm in one of my "spots", . . . one of several locations that I ride my bike to, get out my trumpet and play down by the riverside. My favorite spot this day is taken by sunbathers,. an isolated,. safer area. Fate?

Up around 100th st there is this little jetty that goes out in the river, about 10 feet,. no more. I place my bike right behind me about 5 feet. I've done this at least 30 times.(hence the over confidence that nobody is going to mess with me.) After all, . . . I'm out here playing music,. with my back turned,. in communication with the universe. Nobodies gonna JACK me out here?

Right?

. . . .

WRONG.

THAT SHIT VANISHED.

POOF!,... BUT NO SMOKE.

WAIT! I STILL GOT MY HORN?

I STILL GOT MY WALLET?

Shit ...

You got to be a bad so and so and EVIL to take my shit while I'm playing music,... which I thought meant you CANT take my shit.

IT WAS TAKEN RIGHT UNDER MY NOSE I WAS SO LOST IN MY MUSIC.

A quick survey of the area leaves no clues,... but ANOTHER persons bike just sitting in the open with nobody around.

"Should I take it?,... somebody just TOOK mine."

NAH.

The quickest morality test Ive seen,... man its funny how the world works sometimes.

Now what was my bike getting picked REALLY about? Karma? I was headed for a big accident? I don't need it anymore? Somebody needs it more than me? Questions I had to ask,. which only lead to more questions,... and ONE answer ...

Never get to comfortable in NYC.

Dedicated to the kid I believe did it, . . . oh there IS KARMA for jacking a musician while he's playing to try and tune the world. right?

shit . . .

NYC BEYOND DRAMA 2

Only In New York

Our day begins as I walk from 50th and 10th in Hells kitchen to my job at Sam Ash on 48th between 6th and 7th ave last Thursday. The street is OWNED by kids going to school but I make my way through them screaming all kinds of ridiculous shit to get past the rehab guys on the corner,. having their first of what will be all day long smoke breaks where they talk shit about who smoked more crack. The bodega where I start my day is jammed,. but Amir got my back because I made sure he got his O2 tank. The deal is still intact,. he uses my address,. and in return he hooks me up with street shit,. like the big ass TV I got that he "found" on the street. Amir lives in the basement of the bodega and always lets me go to the front of the line. As I leave 3 kids throw D batteries at me from across the street, but they miss. (heh.)

I get to 9th ave and Hells kitchen becomes midtown and real people are now replaced with tourists who are always lost, confused, with their maps out,. or getting hustled by the tour bus guys who are on every corner. There's a HUGE, ANGRY crowd over by the NY post,. but I don't know why,. (yet). When I get to the street where my job is there's some CRAZY shit,. because I've suddenly been transplanted to a movie set without anybody saying anything. Some guy stops me and says, . . . "wait, . . . shooting", . . . and it turns out the remake of the movie FAME now OWNS the block,. and I have to wait to go in. Picture the movie or TV series Fame. I was in the middle of that shit,. like another twisted version of reality. Once I start work, a singer comes in MAD AS HELL and explains that the post had a cartoon that was anti-Obama,. and that the protest she was at was out for blood. "Al Sharpton is there,. and the post is going down!," she explained . . . "The post has always been some bullshit".,. I said. After selling and talking shit all day,. losing it with some bi-polar

68

woman lecturing me on identity theft,. (music stores bring out the CRAZY people),. I go to get a haircut at my spot, . . . the subway at 40th and 7th ave.Soon as I walk in, . . . the guys declare, . . . "Hey, . . . MARK 6, . . .".a mark 6 is a really expensive,prized saxophone,. and both barber cats have old classics worth a lot of money.Every time I come in I tell them to bring that shit to Sam Ash,. so I can "cop",. but they never do.While they buzz my receding dome with a 1 blade they explain why.One guy has an alto signed by Lou Donaldson and a Japanese business guy has offered him 25,000 G'S . . . I told him,. "Man, . . . stop cutting the little bit of hair I have left and go get paid, . . . that's $25,000." "Man,. $25,000 ain't shit to me, . . . I'll deal with that shit later,. or call my wife and have her check into it".I was crying I laughed so hard, . . . and told him, . . . $25,000 ain't shit?, . . . must be nice,. your just cutting my hair for fun then?

After that I had to go take care of some business, . . . at the Laundromat at 47th and 10th,. and when I get their its jammed up, . . . as this one family has taken the entire left row. "Don't worry honey, . . . I got a machine for you in the back", . . . my friend tells me,. that Ive seen every few weeks for years now,. but we never exchange names.She tells me the usual,. her boss is an asshole,. and shes done with his shit,. but then when he comes in its all smiles and shit, . . . but a wink to let me know, . . . "Isn't he SUCH an asshole?", . . . (no. doubt.)

I don't have a gig, . . . so now its back to my railroad apartment to practice,. and the whole building knows my deal, . . . always finish by 10pm.After I practice its off to bodega land once more,. or my Chinese spot where as soon as I come in,. they get tight because I'm always asking for shit they don't make, . . . like sweet and sour water chestnuts or something, . . . but I gotta switch that $3.75 shit up somehow.

On my way back I see a GIANT ass plant outside the bodega,. just left to die on the street, . . . I'm not having that,. so I take the plant up to my room.She's in a big ass pot,. but needs soil, . . . bad.I name her Bertha.(I'm known for saving art on the street to.).I pass my roommate on the street on his way to get some miller lights,. blue can,. as always.I fade to sleep among a chorus of car alarms,giant trucks rumbling up the street,. and a hisssssssing radiator,. ready to rewind and see whats coming down tomorrow in new york city 2009, ... the last thing I hear is the sound of an alto clarinet in the distance. The trip? This shit is a true story, ... and we write new ones every day.

All 8 million.(or whatever) of us ...

Peace.

NYC BEYOND DRAMA 3

Remember the Chupa Cabra? A few years back,. he was pretty big in the news. Crazy monster that destroyed cows. He had a guest appearance on the X-files,. and was up in Washington Heights on t-shirts as a huge weight-lifter guy with a giant fly head . . .

Right around that time I was walking home in Jackson Heights around 4am after a gig,. and I was being tagged, . . . followed by a car driving behind me real slow. I was being sized up, . . . was I a viable target to get picked? (robbed). I had my bass-clarinet with me,. and I had just charged that shit on a credit card. This was going down in an area with nobody around, . . . I was all alone. "If these guys make a move", . . . I thought.

Sure enough, . . . they pulled up and 3 guys got out,. were they drunk? Couldn't tell. "We need to talk to you", . . . the "leader" said, . . . and they got in my way.

AAHHHHHHHH!!!!! WHAT THE HELL DO YOU WANT?! DON'T YOU KNOW WHO I AM?! YOU MUST BE INSANE TO TALK TO ME. I'M THE CHUPA CABRAS, . . . ILL EAT YOUR HEART RIGHT NOW. RIGHT. NOW. I EAT COWS,. ILL EAT YOU. GIVE ME YOUR BLOOD. RRRARA!

These guys were now thrown off and didn't know what to do,. this was some shit they didn't expect.

AHHHHH! COME ON! I put my stuff down,. and made a move towards one of them like I might attack them and shit,. I yelled some more CRAZY shit then,. ILL BLEED ALL OVER YOU!!! I'M THE CHUPA CABRAS! RRARRHH!!

The leader guy was like, . . . "lets get outta here man,." They got in the car and drove off.I actually found a Cab for the last 2 blocks.My bass-clarinet and I had survived again.

In NYC you gotta learn how to handle survival drama should you catch some.Your going to cross paths with freaks,hustlers,all kinds of stupid scenarios.Ive been having to many confrontations as of late.A fake-security guy trying to flex on some bullshit,. and what I REALLY hate, . . . tourists or people with money thinking I work wherever they are, . . . asking me to do stuff.SOME people think EVERYBODY works for them.

Just tonight in the bodega on the corner of 50th and 10th, . . . I'm getting a vitamin water, . . . I love that stuff.Some guy and his girlfriend come up to me and say, . . . "Let me get a roast beef sandwich,mayo,lettuce,and a turkey sand . . ."

I DON'T WORK HERE MAN, . . . DO I ***?

The guy grabbed his girlfriend and bolted out of there with the QUICK.

Almost like he had just seen . . . THE CHUPA . . . CABRAS . . .

NYC BEYOND DRAMA 4

The Mayor of Homeless Park (Before OBAMA)

At 48th st just off of 8th ave in NYC is a small park area that has been dedicated to a group of local firefighters that lost their lives on 9/11. Its across the street from a bodega that sells $1 pizza slices that really ain't that bad. The park itself is just one small fountain monument,. like 4 feet high, . . . 2 rows of benches,. and about 8 tables with chairs, . . . all bolted to the ground of course. Nobody comes there to take pause for the firefighters, . . . as this park is now run by its Mayor, . . . who's name just so happens to be, . . . "Mayor". I like to take my lunch break there,. and after mayor saw that I was going to be a regular, . . . he explained the rule, . . . mainly, . . . that he and his crew would be there every day, . . . drunk. S'all good with me, . . . this park is a great one to break bread with the SUN around mid-day. (the requisite sky-rats and peeps are there in their eternal struggle for crumbs of course.) Mayors crew is really just 2 other people, . . . a woman who always has earrings on with a beer belly,. (I'm not used to woman beer bellies),. and a guy with dreads that he has wrapped up looking like the crown of thorns from all the Jesus Crucifixion paintings, . . . (his connection to Jesus may be the WINE that Jesus was always turning water into.). Mayors a happy cat, . . . even though he don't have many teeth left at his proclaimed age of 35.(?) . . . He's always laughing and talking loud about something,. revealing his low-income grill.

What got me thinking about MAYOR was his OBAMA tee shirt that he wears all the time. OBAMA shirts are in bodegas all over town, . . . cheap,. over sized shirts of his face and many with speech quotes, . . . and the required CHANGE WE CAN BELIEVE IN. I can get with that, . . . since GHOULIANI,. the ex-mayor of new york is about the saddest excuse for a human being on the face of the Earth to me.

Whats incredible here to me, . . . is that OBAMA has made a CONNECTION TO THE STREET. The street has found a way to profit off his message, . a message their down with. Who is this guy that he can pull this off?

I asked mayor about why he was pro-Obama, . . . and his response was quick and decisive, . . . great for a debate exchange.

"I EXIST . . . OBAMA MEANS THAT I EXIST".

Ok then, . . . I heard OBAMA likes TRANE.

Perfect music to SAVE THE WORLD.

NYC BEYOND DRAMA 5

ARTIST PUNCHES OUT TOURIST

New York City Times Square can be a strange place to see the human race in action.

Just above where they drop the ball on new years eve,. near "m&m land",. is a strip of Times Square where artists draw portraits or cartoons of tourists for as low as $5. They sit there and draw and draw all day long. I like to see if there accurate as the tourists are either bored,scared,or both . . . scared and bored.(tourists are some strange people in general.).I thought of trying to be a portrait person myself having some art-chops back in the day,. and having tried being a street musician more than once.

Maybe later . . .

I'm crossing the front of artists row and I see a tourist standing up, . . . irate,. holding a new portrait up, . . .

"THIS IS CRAP!!" "I LOOK NOTHING LIKE THIS!!".

"AS AN ARTIST,. YOU SUCK!!".

And the kicker, . . .

"I'M NOT PAYING!!" . . .

I tried to catch a view of the portrait as people started to stop and watch this "must be times square entertainment" . . .

The artist, . . . "You DARE insult my work?!!?"

POW!!!!!

ARTIST PUNCHES OUT TOURIST.

Nobody saw it coming,. and nobody did shit.

Tourist DOWN.

KNOCKED OUT.

FACE DOWN.

"Police!!,. Police!!, . . . someone shouted.

A Times Square cop strolled up,. all slow,. and not interested, . . .

Cop to the artist, . . . "Why did you hit him?"

I kept going, . . . having gotten what I knew would be a blog,. and left the cop to handle the situation, . . . clearly he was "New York's finest" . . .

Do I like violence? no, . . . but a small part of me took pleasure that in toady's world,. I caught a case of . . .

ARTISTS REVENGE.

BEYOND DRAMA 1

In 1978,. Divorce was no way near as popular as it is today in 2011. When my parents sat my brother and I down and explained that our family was over we just sat and cried and cried. I was 8,. my brother 7,. and we didn't really understand just why our world was over,. gone. I remember swimming the next day and refusing to get out of the water,. as I came up with a solution to my problem . . . sadness

I decided to EAT myself into OBLIVION.

Being FAT was also not as popular than as is today where Hip Hop has somehow made it part of their culture. I would grow to become tortured over my,. um . . . condition . . . complete with memories that will last a lifetime.

I started right away,. going for everything I could get to,. starting with Hot Dogs and Donuts,. scaring my Mom a little bit. It didn't take long to become the FAT kid,. the fattest kid at Pine Tree elementary. I remember being weighed in Gym and the whole class falling out laughing when my weight was announced 60 pounds above everyone else. I lost friends,. good ones,. right away as they were embarrassed to be near me. One was named Terrance. I went from an all star in little league to the fat catcher who grounds out or flies out,. straight out of the film,. the Bad News Bears. The biggest humiliations were soon to come.

The one that's the strongest in my mind was somehow associated with CHURCH. My confirmation into the Catholic Church. First,. during preparation for the ceremony I was paired with a girl from the other side of the room. This was a random selection. When the girl found out I was to be her partner,. she started CRYING and had to be consoled by her girlfriends. I heard them telling her how they would ask for a switch,. and I couldn't even look at them.I felt so low.Then,. after mad family drama to get me a suit that fit,. I met the bishop for a photograph.I'll never forget how he was taken aback,. shocked to see how FAT I was.He was to late to hide a reaction.The photos would haunt me for years.

It was MIDDLE SCHOOL where my drama would force me to the bottom of the sea,. where the pressure caused me to fight back,. and fight for my life.

Just before I left for that school,. I was at a baseball game way out in the outfield,. and I caught what should have been a home run by accident.It was a hit by ROBERT GREENE,. The only black cat in school.He ran out to the Field and said,. "You and me Fat boy!,. right now!".I didn't fight back,. and I had an enemy now waiting to fight me at every turn.Greene would torture me with his shit,. but not as bad as this girl who used to follow me around school going,. "FUCK YOU YOU FAT PIECE OF SHIT".Man,. she followed me around with this shit all the time.I never looked back at her and believed that I was a fat piece of shit. Then it was Frank DeGenero,. who would Slap me in the face every day! This stuff was adding up,. and when my grandparents died,. and then my mom had Brain Surgery,. in which My father gave me a letter she wrote to read after she died,. I finally had enough.My mom survived,. and somehow on my own I had reached the shatterpoint.

ENOUGH.

I was avoiding Gym (Greene was there)by making appointments with the guidance counselor every time I had to go,. and he wasn't buying it,. so I was eventually forced to fight back Greene.We had to play catch or something and he tried to get me to fight again,. and I remember looking him in the eye and throwing the ball back trying to destroy him. Eventually he went away.(Another kid fought back and the school got involved).My real problem was my eating routine:

Wake up and have a full breakfast,tons of cereal at home.Go to school and have a full school breakfast.Have 2 lunches,especially with Dipsy Doodles corn chips,and orange drink.Head home.More Cereal,. tons.Coffee cake,. Ice cream . . . tons,PIE,and then bugging my mom about dinner. As much dinner as I could stuff,. Chicken skin! And then ice cream again to finish.

Somehow I cut all that out and was eating celery like crazy. Passing out from exercise. It took me a few months but I improvised a diet and exercise thing,. and got rid of a big part of the weight. My father sued my mother for custody and the judge let my brother and I decide. Trying to transform myself at the time from being fat,. I moved in with my father as part of the process,. causing problems with my relationship with my Mother that would take years to repair. I wouldn't reach somewhat normal shape until I was 17. That same year ACNE turned me into what I would be called,. "PIZZA".

Such is life,. and I have battled weight ever since,. going up and down again as much as 60 pounds. Working with food was always dangerous,. especially the whole "Sandwich artist" trip,. making sandwiches at Subway. Free cookies and soda. I have studied food and myself with a limited degree of success applying what I've learned to real time application. All of this is related to Sex in a way,. a very complicated issue that I have also studied and looked for guidance on. Eating is a sexual experience in a way,. and I am a selfish person. I never became an exercise freak, but I have dabbled in gyms and Yoga. Bike riding,. especially the NYC Bike path on the west side,. has been my saving grace. If I'm addicted to anything,. its music . . . I play music as much as possible,. and if I was eating all the time I've been practicing the last 20 years,. I would be dead.

With me I took the humiliation more than anything else. The way the kids treated me. When people judge you as being lesser of a person based on how you look,. it tends to become part of your psyche. (Old news in 2011). All though I forgave myself long ago,. part of me will always be,.

THE FAT KID.

I still waddle.

BEYOND DRAMA 2

I have had so many jobs trying to survive,. and been in so many ridiculous situations because of it.No Different than many folks who like to eat food and sleep in beds.In High school I worked at the local Supermarket,. the A&P,unloading trucks and stocking shelves. No drama there.The Beyond drama is when I joined the NIGHT SHIFT a few years later when I was trippin',. trying to figure out just who the hell I was.Turns out that I would find myself quite close to the STREET throughout my life.The STREET is where those things happen in life when we just lose control of even our most basic reasoning,and the fun part of life begins.Years later a close friend of mine who knew the street quite well said he felt like my true self had an understanding of it.Here's how it all began.

Crazy Joe gave me the job.Joe and I had history.He was about 400 pounds and drank like a fish.Bald,thick glasses,and Loud.I drove him crazy destroying his apple juice display and fucking with him over the intercom screaming "GGGOOODDDMOORNNINGG JOEE SARUUBO!",.After seeing the movie good morning Vietnam with Robin Williams(MORK),. who I would meet in person one day.Joe gave me the Night Shift.

Working at Night,. from 11pm to 7am is a direct challenge of nature.The basic nature of reality suggests that when the Sun goes down,. you sleep in the dark.You have to also figure out what to do on your nights off.As your sleep pattern falls into disarray,. and for me,. a growing problem with breathing while I did sleep,. Sleep Apnea,. you start to lose touch with reality and start creating a new one,. a DARK one.At one point shit go so weird I thought I saw ghosts and even hid in a Pizza Parlor across the street from my apartment on main st in Nyack New York.(Where they had a video game I used to play before they went extinct.)

When I joined the staff,. they all made more money than me,. but they put me on register AND wanted me to finish as much work as they did,. packing out the shelves. That in itself was pissing me off. When we came in there would be huge stacks of stuff everywhere and our job of course was to price it all and put it all on the shelf. Dog and Cat food was my biggest responsibility,. TONS.

But,. that's not the Darkness I'm talking about. I'm talking about when DRUGS enter the equation. Drugs at work is of course insane,. but when the whole staff, including the supervisor is in on this shit,. your now a member of a dark world where priorities are all in reverse.

It started simply enough,. just some WEED. On breaks,. and before everybody drove home. I didn't smoke with them,. I just observed. My boss drove me home High,. a little scary,. but it was a ride home,. so I took it. (This kind of compromise would be taken to extremes in later years in NYC). Another guy at work,. just married with a new child,. would also give me rides and drive REALLY REALLY FAST,. scaring the shit out of me. I was to green to see that he was on COKE. Another coke head on staff helped me fix the starter on this busted ass 1978 pickup truck I found myself with.

Oh yeah . . . COCAINE.

Cocaine took everything to the level known as next. The deal was a simple one. A dealer comes in with coke for the guys and in return takes whatever he wants from the store. TONS of shit. My instructions were simple,. DON'T SAY SHIT. On register, I had to look the other way. The guys changed . . . acting crazy and doing crazy shit,. like throwing tuna cans and big glass mayonnaise jars over the aisles at random. Not funny,. weird and dangerous. I had to watch out that I didn't get hit by this shit. The boss would even page me over the store intercom: "Matt,. bring straws to the bakery". The bakery was our special meeting place. When they got down with their shit,. I got down with the chicken wings,. and whatever else I decided I wanted to eat. One time I ate nothing but Macadamia nuts for days. Sounds like I was on it, but I just got off on having an entire supermarket of food to choose from. The darkness for me you see, was not using,. it was the decision to TAKE ADVANTAGE of this environment.

Simply,. I decided to make money off of their madness. I started making offers to customers coming in: "Give me $50 cash,. and take whatever the fuck you want,. I wont stop you".

I started getting PAID from this,. and scared more than one girlfriend when their boyfriends took advantage of my special deal. The freaks came out at night. Then,. to escalate,. I had a friend pull up in a van at 4am,. when I would LOAD up on stolen shit. Cases of beer, cases of cigarettes,. that I would sell for profit at home.

What I didn't know,. was that the coke guy that gave me the crazy rides was stealing cases of cigarettes like crazy all ready and the store was watching him. He got caught by an undercover security guy and went to JAIL for this shit. I found out later that he went back on Coke when he got out,. started speeding again,. got into a car accident and DIED. I was THAT close to DEATH.

BUT,. once he went down,. the rest of the guys decided they were in the clear and went back to coke every night,. except one guy,. who was next to me in aisle 9 and drove a truck,. that graduated to full blown CRACK. He was cooking it up in the seafood department every night. Shit got so out I started walking around with a big HAMMER to defend myself.

Then,. more shit hit the proverbial fan.

Something went down between the dealer and the guys,. and the dealer called the cops and said,. "Everyone at the A&P right now is on Coke". I was up front when a cop came in,. and blocked the doors. He told me to give him the intercom and said,. "This is the police. We have blocked the exit. Everyone on staff at the store come to front right now."

We lined up,. and then we were checked for drugs,. and threatened with a strip search. The guys had just used,. but didn't have any on them,. just INSIDE them. I was clean ... (Did they know about my $50 program?).The worst was that an old Haitian cat,. Brunnel,. that did the floors,. was interrogated as well.Brunnel was a religious and clean person,. and he was crying when he was put through this shit,. as he had a family on the line.The cops left,. but warned us we were being watched.

Seeing what happened to Brunnel shook me up.Shortly after this I was in the middle of my biggest heist ever,. 2 carts of stuff,. when I suddenly came to reality and asked myself,. just what the HELL was I doing? I put everything back,. and stopped all my $ schemes,. reborn.

But the Coke and Crack thing was still going full blast.They even survived an undercover security check with a tip off.

A new guy on the crew and I decided to BLOW the SPOT,. and we DRY-SNITCHED. Everybody was busted and fired.I worked a little more,. helping Brunnel and practicing my trumpet on breaks,. but I had enough and found a job at a place called TOWER RECORDS.I'll never forget how cold the manager at the A&P was when I told him I was leaving.BRRRR . . .

TOWER would be a whole other world.Something that could only happen then in the 90's,. as I write this post Towers bankruptcy in 2006.Another story for another day . . .

The STREET however,. remains with me.

BEYOND DRAMA 3

If you fall off the path that is meant for you,. you can suffer a terrible price to be re-adjusted,. or realigned. Who I am,. who I'm supposed to be was a Far Cry from the life I was living in my early 20's. My father of course felt I should live life one way,. and the person I was to become,. the person I didn't really know,. was simply not capable of it. I tried to go college for art and then realized that music was my calling. I tried to go to music school,. but had no money. I was all ready bankrupt from an impossible medical bill from when my right knee was so bad I couldn't walk and I forced into surgery. I was working 2 jobs and trying to understand it all when my Father decided if I was late with the rent I had to go. Out of money, out of luck, I went to NYC,. 40 minutes a way and got a room at the Jersey City YMCA . . . 40 minutes on the path train stop to Penn station. Ironically,. My father helped me move in to this insane place even seeing the vibe. It was a power struggle with his marriage and I had no power,. so . . . I was about to be introduced to LIFE in a strange new way,. entering a strange new world.

We drove down in my 78 Datsun Red pickup truck that leaked Gas and had a shifting engine block. The liner in the back was stolen. As agreed,. my dad sold it to some Dominican guys that shipped it to D.R. I had discovered this magical YMCA in the Village Voice which had an add that said,. "Starving artists and musicians,. come to New York . . ." They said they had a room and I packed up my shit and hoped for the best.

When I arrived I discovered the place was in the Ghetto. No white folks,. and lots of thuggery. I was scoped upon entry for opportunities. What could be gotten off me? How easy a mark was I? Turns out the only room available was one that a Drunk had lived in,. and he had spent years PISSING IN THE CLOSET. Staff was not feeling me. I had all my shit with me and was told that I was on the worst floor in the building for drugs and crazy shit. I left a note in big letters for the eventual break in a few days later while I was at work at Tower Records at Lincoln center NYC.

TOUCH MY SHIT AND DIE. ANYONE THAT TAKES MY SHIT I WILL FIND YOU AND KILL YOU. STRAIGHT UP. YOU WILL DIE IF YOU TOUCH MY SHIT.

One night of course on the jacked up elevator a crackhead told me,. "I got your message about touching your shit",. and he got off. hmm ...

I ran into an older, dignified black cat later on and he told me to get to the 7th floor,. where he was in charge and controlled the mayhem. He even went downstairs with me and made the staff hook me up. Later that day I went down to the office to switch keys.

When I walked in I found a man I never saw in a tie carving a Giant Turkey! Homeboy had 2 hookers with him to boot! He was all smiles as we switched keys and he got back to his crazy thanksgiving summer party. WTF? I said goodbye to some weirdo I loaned 20 bucks to in the bathroom and also the deadbeat Dad that was one the run from the law for bad child support,. and moved up to 7th heaven,. 2 doors down from my saviour,. EUGENE. The 7th floor is the heart of this beyond drama,. I saw so much shit. Like characters in a play for the insane,. let me introduce you to them.

GENE.

Eugene ran the floor to a degree. As soon as he saw me I was invited to visit and discovered he had 2 rooms in one and his spot had everything. Big TV and VCR,. the rage at the time. Nice clothes,. he was hooked up and explained he had been their a long time. A working telephone was the thing,. and I had to hook up a number as soon as possible for myself. Turns out that Gene was not only a great Jazz singer,. (I was a fledgling trumpet player), but a preacher for something called A COURSE IN MIRACLES. An early version of meta-physical Catholicism. Gene wanted me to study with him and invited me to his church. I went twice.

Gene and I hung out and became buddies and I'll never forget the positive things we got into.Gene got me a bike and we would ride in the village in NYC all over on Friday and Saturday nights where he knew everyone.We stopped to talk to a vendor who tried to sell us porn.Gene said,. "What am I supposed to do with this shit?" . . . "You know damn well what to do!",. his friend said.I used the bike to make jam sessions at Smalls near the Village Vanguard where my hero Trane used to play and I used to play the jam session until Sunrise.Leaving in the bright sun,. I vividly remember the trash and one gay guy telling another one,. "I just got fucked".One time on the way back I stopped at a homeless shelter to eat . . . I wasn't doing to good then.Gene and I always stayed tight,. and he was worried after having sex with a woman that he later found out had AIDS from a lower floor.

"You remind me of my grandfather",. she told him as they made love.

We went to jam sessions together and at Mo Betta's he floored the audience.He was great. Gene had 2 sons he was always getting calls from and he said I was his third son.In our last phone conversation after I left,. and told him my roommate Girlfriend was stinking up my towels,. Gene said "I love you man." I'll always remember him as he described himself in a story about him and the great tenor player Booker Ervin when they would smoke weed after playing all night . . . "Booker said I was a nice cat." Now the one person Gene couldn't take,. was the guy in the room between us,. STEVE.On with the play . . .

STEVE

Whatever happened to Steve,. he was on a mission to CHANT it away,. and chant he did. Night and day,. he was the one.He chanted with his door open and incense flowing out.He tried to get me to join him,. but I never subscribed to his proposed version of Buddhism,. and that whole non-attachment thing.Back then I wasn't even attached to myself.I tried to jam some blues with Steve on his little keyboard but we didn't have anything happening. Steve never could understand why Gene didn't like him,. but he was ok about it,. just needed to KEEP CHANTING.Across the hall was LEO.Leo was far,far from being a Lion in any sense of the word.He was a living tragedy.

LEO

Leo was an old white gut that couldn't walk. He had crutches and was forced to drag himself to the bathroom where he would literally just SHIT everywhere. We had one bathroom for the floor and had to share. When Leo would destroy it,. Gene would end up cleaning it since the staff wouldn't respond for days. Leo should have been in a home. The few times we talked he said,. "No family,. no friends". I heard he had cancer,. and he would just lie in bed all day cooking,. in a prison of some kind. Once a day,. a church came and brought him food. What can you do?

NO NAME.

No name was a 20 something black cat on the run from the law. "Better if you don't know my name man". He was high on something,. maybe life . . . he was quite positive despite his, . . . shall we say,. adversity. One night at 3 or 4 am,. he knocked on my door like crazy. "SUGAR!!!" "SUGAR!!!" . . . Turned out that NN had bad Diabetes and was having a reaction. I gave him my ice tea mix and he shoveled it down his throat throwing the dust everywhere. "THANKS MAN". NN was part of a great hook-up,. and a literal one. Before I got a phone,. NN tapped into the building line in the hallway and showed me how to get make free calls. I called EVERYONE,. Long distance and the like. Coming off the elevator one day,. I was met by the PHONE POLICE. I of course didn't know anything about whatever freaks were tapping the line.

THE GUY THAT DIED.

One day I came off the elevator and found BLOOD going to the right. I never went right,. but followed the trail in case I could help someone. I found an old man sitting down in his room with Blood on the floor. He had blood clots in his legs and had cut himself. I asked if I could help,. and he said no. I went down and told the staff anyway and figured they would act. They didn't and homeboy DIED. I found out of course coming off the elevator the next day when someone said,. "So and so died,. go get some shit!" . . . The YMCA people where all taking the stuff in his room. The blood stains in the hallway lasted for weeks!

OTHER MEMORIES INCLUDE:

Fat gay dude always hitting on me at the water fountain,. even when I tried to act tough . . . White dude that bleached his room 3 times a day and never spoke to anyone,. CURLY,. this crazy old guy always in a robe and bare feet because he had NEVER EVER CUT HIS TOE NAILS EVER,. and then BOOKS,. a tall,skinny black dude that had thousands of books in his room and claimed to have read them all. On the street there was a guy always playing violin outside staring at me,. and another guy who didn't have a job and always made me stop and listen to his problems and how bad they had become. What could I do?

As the curtain started to close on my Jersey city play of madness,. I remember the view on the roof:Manhattan in all its glory.I used to go up there and practice during sunset,. my favorite time of day.Sometimes old guys would be out there playing cards.Before I left,. there was an anti-abortion protest thing happening every day at a clinic across the street from the building.My initial room gave me a big time view of this special place.

In true Jersey city Y style,. I left in the middle of night without paying,. and out the back door.I went to live with a beautiful Bi-sexual woman that looked like Janet Jackson on the upper west side.My NYC initiation,. and BEYOND DRAMA 3 had met en end.I lasted 6 months.

I'll never forget this early SOURCE OF SOUL.

BEYOND DRAMA 4

In order to survive as a Jazz musician for the last 20 years,. I have not always had an easy go of it.I have had all kinds of jobs,. and for the most part,. they have been 40 hours a week. With no college degree,(which doesn't mean what it used to these days anyway),I have been stuck on the lower tier by and large the entire time,. somehow making the time to still exist as the musician.Some of these jobs where just,. different.

U Ulster county
A Association of
R Retarded
C Citizens

UARC was where I found myself on a self-imposed NYC exile when the music just wasn't working out.I left NYC to start my own business as a yes,. a psychic,in collaboration with a good friend of mine.We had a store to sell and work out of and in 3 months,. we were done.(Stay tuned for this drama)

I was scrambling,. and UARC hired me as an assistant to work with the retarded folks at various work sites for minimum wage.I had just been a Subway sandwich artist and a clerk at a big retail chain called Caldor,. and was led to believe I was being hired as a supervisor at more money.

At Subway the only tale to tell was I gained 40 pounds,. and had to switch to sweat pants. Free cookies and soda did me in more than the giant sandwiches I would improvise.I recall in a nutshell,. a UPS guy that wanted to fight me,working with a pregnant former heroin addict who had a jeri-curl that lived with her mom that hit on me all the time,the 2 old white misers that ran the place,(one named Jerry that lost his business in some kind of scam),the young supervisors always messing with me,the customer that called me stupid that I tried to climb over the counter to fight,Jerry making me save my gloves,an older white lady supervisor that didn't trust me for some reason,and my giant LeBaron car breaking down all the time,with a bad starter,one time in the middle of nowhere during a snowstorm,and lastly,. a car accident in the same car when I did a "Donut",and was left up on a bank of snow.

Back to ARC,.

They sent to me an an electrical company to help the guys recycle parts,. and I met the supervisor . . . a sweet but stressed out woman named Gwen.All I did was work the line with the guys,. not really assist,. and it was brutal physical labor.I called the office saying I thought I was a supervisor and they transferred me to another assistant job helping clean a school for kids who had even worse problems,. such as blindness,being crippled,not being able to speak,. all extreme adversity.Eventually they gave me the supervisor spot there and I got tight with the janitor Vince,. and did most of the work myself.I had to pick all the workers up and drive them home.I remember the principal,. Francine,. who was tough but cool.I was then dispatched to Mohonk mountain,. a resort for rich people.I was to run the dishroom.It reminded me of THE SHINING.The staff didn't trust me,. after finding me watching TV in the lounge on a break.The pace was HECTIC,. as the machine never stopped.I was later dispatched to a recycling plant where we had a literal pit that I stood in filled with used bottles and canisters.We had a giant conveyor belt and had to separate glass,plastic,and more,. and then make huge bails.I was then dispatched again to supervise a McDonalds thruway rest stop cleaning crew,. which meant cleaning the bathrooms.I was getting fat again on free Mcdonalds and one of the other supervisors was a crazy pro gun-pro-america guy with a new wife and son who had a habit of locking his baby in his car by accident.Changing the ketchup dispenser sucked.Later I was dispatched to BARD college to supervise their Dishroom,. another crazy job.Rich College kids are slobs in general and cleaning up after them sucked even more than the previous dishrooms.Did I mention that when I was in college back in the day that my job was running THAT Dishroom? (I need to write a song called dishroom).I recall trying to clean the machine once between Lunch and Dinner and the FUNK was THICK.**FLASHBACK:I met an African woman in New Paltz that worked with me and one time we made love instead of washing dishes**.Back to BARD,. I had a crazy staff,and the Bard people thought I was to tough,. and especially mean to take away one guy's Karaoke machine and microphone during a busy shift and hand him a stack of plates.Then there was the seizures,. UFFA! Eventually I became the assistant manager of this whole community based affair and spent most of my time driving around these huge vans,. in fact getting into an accident and smashing one up pretty bad before I quit and went back to NYC.(I had met a good friend at a jam session near Bard who offered me a room and a way back in).

All of this riff raff and succotash and grits doesn't amount to a hill of beans really.What matters is the folks I met along the way.Mentally challenged they may have been,. but that doesn't mean their hearts weren't filled with GOLD.Sheila was my QUEEN.

SHEILA GREENE

Sheila was really something.Sheila started life being thrown from a window in the projects,. and landing on her head.As tenacious as she was even that early in life,. she survived.She was about 5 foot 2 inches,. 110 pounds,. and could bench press a battleship.She called me "Mack" . . .

"Mack?", . . . "Mack?" . . . You know I like you Mack,. caus,. caus you know I know how to do the work! . . ."

She was my Michael Jordan and really kicked ass on the front of the line at Bard.I told her she was my number one.650 trays in 2 hours and Sheila refused gloves,. getting funk in her hair.She would sound on anyone to slow to keep up,. especially this poor cat named Earl who wore the biggest glasses I ever seen.

"Stupid EARL!! DON'T KNOW WHAT THE FUCK HES DOIN THAT EARL!"

Sheila suffered from mood swings and could cry from being sad or being happy on a dime. She had a full blown relationship with another ARC guy,. a white dude that thought he was black and always had giant winter hats on in the summer.I knew they had sex when Sheila said,."Mack,. Ive been pushin the Bush! Pushin the bush I was mack!".She would talk to herself out loud,. asking and answering questions like that Lord of the Rings creature obsessed with the RING.Nothing gave Sheila more joy than giving presents,. (and buying really big furniture!.)

The presents part had a dark side,. as she would STEAL to give them away.One time after I gassed up the van I found a case of chocolate bars next to my seat that she stole. "Gonna make you Fat Mack!".Then another time she was busted in the living room of the president of the college!! Sheila was mad sad when I left,. and I hope she's still being her,. kicking ass and taking names,. wherever she is.

James Milner.James was a friend who loved the Knicks and singing the song,. "Men in Black" all the time.He always wanted me to "cut the radio on".ARC sent James with me to all the sites,. so he became one of my cleaning soldiers.He always had a smile,and was always ready to go,. EVERY time.Good cat.About 12 in his mind,. 40 in real life.

Ray Ray was another guy that called me "Mack",. and we battled.It as like asking a 9 year old to be on point.We would argue and he would challenge me.Ray Ray had a sense of humor and we had a Saturday job setting up a giant BINGO session at some church.He was always saying to me and laughing,."Bad hair day Mack?" I remember pointing to a scuff on the floor that he missed and asking him what happened.

Ray Ray stepped over it and hid the scuff with his foot.

"I don't know what your talking about Mack."

These kind of memories go on and on.RITA cornering the manager at Bard in his office SCREAMING about the weather,. BILL, who was a normal guy but had a terrible head injury from a motorcycle accident and just couldn't focus, and then this guy EUGENE that had a grand-mal Seizure on me,. so I had to take him to the hospital.

I remember a telephone Psychic told me I would get an "unusual job but that it would work out". I had no idea that I would go on to have the most notorious job in America,. the telephone psychic.

Hmmm . . .

BEYOND DRAMA 5

Almost no person in America doesn't know the name MISS CLEO.

When asked,most people remember her as the first famous telephone psychic,and that she went down on fraud.

I don't know where she is now,but I know she made a lot of bread.In Cleo's wake an entire industry was created that lasts until today in 2011.It's in fact bigger than ever.Just google the word psychic and enter an entire sub culture of millions of people seeking what most likely they will not find.Some will find what they want,escape and validation,or a cure from lonliness or belief in a fantasy future.It can get complicated.

You see,. I speak from personal experience as a bonafide telephone psychic for an entire year.I've had many a strange job over the years,but nothing will over top this one.I could write a whole a book on what went down,but I have to much music to make.

I had lots of validation when I left Sam Ash music in Times Square.MUSIC was the main objective.I wanted time to work on my music,and 40 hours a week selling trumpets wasn't cutting it.I'm sure all the other psychics out there have delicious readings,I mean reasons,why they got into the BIZ.Sounds like I was into some darkness right? I was.I sacrificed myself so that I could live.I put myself up on my own cross seeking salvation from the dark side,and absolution of my mad musical and spiritual quest to be.I met a cat named QUEST once,. and his mission was to have as many BABIES as he could.

Making your own schedule and working from home is a pretty could draaawwwww . . . (like a hit of weed).I had a friend that I explored the spiritual side of life with for years,. my

94

friend to this day. We were deep into the metaphysical,. and I had studied Astrology, Tarot cards, and numerology for years. I had given people readings, just being me, so getting paid for it seemed like a novel idea,. and my friend was having a great success at it. She pushed me in.

I still didn't know if I could even do it though . . . REALLY. Could I see information about a person based only on their voice? Can I help them REALLY? WITHOUT Bullshitting? To do this kind of thing you have to really believe in it,. truly believe you had "the gift". My "gift" was all technical things that I found truth in,. the Astrology and beyond,. I was into Native American totems then,. still am.

So I had to be "tested."

I figured that,. if I passed the 2 tests,. reading the staff,. and was offered the job, than maybe I could find another way to make my life in my NYC Rent control on 50th and 10th ave make sense. I passed these tests to my surprise and then tried to make their minimum hours while keeping my 40 hours at the music store and still working on music, playing gigs all over town. My system broke down, and with the psychic thing actually working I made a VITAL mistake,. and decided that this was my new direction. As an Aries,. I risked it all, quit Sam Ash, and made an impossible job my only source of income. Some people out there really made this work as a career,. and some where even RICH off this madness.

In the beginning I learned you have to have your phone on 24/7 to build up your following. I had much to learn . . . The first agency had TV ads and was known all over the country. I was on a staff of about 150, and we worked round the clock. I was making about the same money I was at the store in about 24 hours . . . cool. But I was soon being looked at for not getting return customers. I ended up getting involved in so much crazy shit. I remember a man who couldn't accept his wife leaving him, and a rich guy calling me from the train every day to talk racquetball equipment. A woman who was a cop in NYC and was having a hard time with responsibility of supervising 200 men. Gay cats called with drama. Most of the calls where woman involved with married men. I just went on raw instinct, and actually helped people on many occasions.

My official stats for this line where 5,551 minutes, which is 92.5 hours, and then right after a bonus for hours, I was shocked to get this:

> Dear Matt,
>
> While we have appreciated your service with us, due to your low call statistics coupled with our evaluation results, it is in the best interests of both parties to discontinue our relationship.
>
> And after I pressed further: My negative testimonials. (I lost the good ones,. about 10 of them, . . . Really!)

"Matt's voice came across as warm, very spiritual, and a bit intimidating. He speaks on a very intellectual and spiritual realm, so he can be a bit hard to understand for someone not savvy about the metaphysical realm. He is extremely knowledgeable and very inspirational to listen to. He has an air of wisdom about what he speaks about and he's very in tune with his spirit guides . . .

Throughout the reading, I did feel his pace was a bit slow when answering a question and he explained in a way that was a bit hard to understand, due to the fact that he is a highly intellectual reader. He strongly and quickly honed in on the subject of interest. He does, at times, get sidetracked in the reading when answering questions because he has a strong tendency to be a bit preachy.

I asked him about matters of love/relationships and money/finance. Overall, I felt his abilities were stronger in the area of destiny/life path. He has a profound sense of higher wisdom that can be very educational and therapeutic for a caller that needs deep spiritual and emotional guidance. One criticism though, he does not give as many details and information about the situation as some other psychics.

"He waited for me to say something. He said his name and extension and that is it. Not, 'do you have a question' or 'How can I help you?' He didn't ask for my name.

I had a career question for Matt but it took a weird turn. It was answering questions I didn't ask, and only half answering questions I did ask. He answered my specific questions but the answers were vague or broad. I feel that he was guessing some of the answers as the answers didn't feel right. I didn't feel like I was any further ahead or in a better direction than I was prior to asking.

*   *   *

Cant get any more honest with you than that. I was fired. Along the way I did get a $1,000 bonus for time logged on.

Now I had to move quickly as the perspective in my life had changed with the quick. I was now living in upstate New York, about an hour from the city. I signed on with a new agency, as I now knew what the deal was, and knew I could actually do this.

Here's my profile from the second site:

Matt

CALL

I'm available now!
Call me at
1-886-MY-ASTRO

Extension: 4155

Approval Rating:

Rate: 3.00 USD/3.40 CAD

Consultations on PsychicCenter.com: 388

Expertise: Clairaudience, Clairsentience, Numerology, Astrology, Native American Medicine Cards and Tarot reading

Call: <u>1 866 692 7876</u>

Enter: Ext 4155 and talk to me!

My first profound psychic experience occurred in 1990. It was the one I could not ignore. During a meditation, I was contacted by a musician, the deceased brother of a good friend. I have worked with many spirit guides since and have practiced as a professional psychic for over 14 years. The psychic and metaphysical gifts are strong in my family. I like to begin a reading with empathic messages. In addition, I will use many other methods of divination such as Astrology and Medicine cards (Native American Tarot that put us in touch with our animal spirit guides). During a reading, I inevitably gets messages from the spirit world to help you gain perspective and assist you through the changes that Life brings. I believe a reading should be fun and empowering. I look forward to your call.

Available:

Monday, Tuesday, Thursday: 8:00 a.m. - 1:00 p.m. and 6:00 p.m. - 11:00 p.m. PST

Getting to know   Feedback

[i] Getting to know Matt

Ever wanted to meet your favorite advisor? Get to know her or him a bit better? From time to time we will bring you interviews with PsychicCenter advisors. Here is where you can read how they found out what special gifts they have, how they developed their skills, and why we think they are so good at guiding us on our life path. If this interview inspires you, just give them a call.

How and when did you first find out about your 'psychic abilities'?

I discovered my psychic abilities in 1990. During a meditation I was contacted by the brother of a very good friend, a deceased musician named Frank. When I was playing at a concert, not long after the meditation, I found I could channel Frank through music.

How was it growing up with these special skills. Are they natural talents or did you study and develop them?

I was 20 when I began studies in Astrology with my aunt who was a master Astrologer. I studied in metaphysics with another psychic. It was a combination of natural (every psychic has a unique version of the gift) and actual technical study of Astrology, Tarot, and Numerology for me.

Do you think anyone can develop psychic skills?

We are entering a time where everyone is going to have increased access to our natural abilities. Psychics arrived first to show that it's possible and help others to discover their own abilities. It is all about where someone is in their own evolution, and what they believe and know is possible.

What type of mentality do you think it takes to develop these skills?

Thoughts create reality: which I first remembered by reading the Seth books by Jane Roberts. You have to know that what you are doing is possible, learn to trust yourself and, above all, to not be afraid (tame the ego!)

Are you able to turn your psychic abilities 'on' or 'off' when you want to? Do you have any rituals to turn them 'on'.

I find the environment and people I'm around affect the degree to which my abilities open. It is situational. If I get a message or information that is meant for someone, it is almost impossible for me not to reveal it. I act as a translator when doing readings, and, at times, a guardian of sacred information because there are times when I get information that neither I nor the client actually asked for.

How did you get into doing psychic readings?

I began to read not long after the channeling meditation. As information came through, I simply relayed it. It is about getting a real connection to the person and then getting them the information they need, the information they are allowed to receive in order to help them gain perspective and move on their current situation. As my spirit guide Lucinda says, "As a psychic you are a spirit guide in the flesh."

What happens during a psychic reading?

Both the Psychic and client open to take a closer look at an issue. The opening involves clairaudience (hearing), clairsentience (feeling and knowing). I use Astrology and the Tarot. This gives even greater information and meaning. I also like the Medicine Cards for contacting animal spirit guides.

What is your primary tool for divination? What is your specialty?

I am my main tool. In other words, I like to start the reading with my own psychic take on the situation, not using any outside tools. The tools will tell me if they can help or have something to add and I follow their lead if they wish to present an idea. Every reading is unique. Sometimes spirit guides or even deceased loved ones may come to help out or deliver a message, although it does not happen every time. Speaking with spirit guides is one of my unique gifts, with my primary objective to deliver the message.

Can you communicate with spirits who have passed on?

It does happen on occasion, and always with a very specific reason. Every time I have been a part of that experience, it has been to relieve a distressed emotional state in the client. More often than not, the person here may be having trouble with loss, guilt, and/or depression. A message from the other side can be very uplifting.

Is there anything else you'd like to share about your abilities or a good experience?

Please give me a call! Try the Medicine Cards. The animal spirit guides have a great sense of honesty and they are tenacious. It can be fun. I believe we are here to learn and evolve. Let us try and do that together.

Just now looking through my notebook from this session,. I was getting pretty good at this,but I still wasn't making enough money.I was making like $150 to $350 a week,and it was driving me crazy.I had one lady that called me every day looking for help to get money from rich men with her own twisted perspective.Who was more twisted,. her?,or me for being her psychic?

Eventually I left this site for a site based in France that was talking big bucks,. using a chat-room style with a web cam method that was paying way more.I hedged all my bets on this one,. the top of my psychic mountain.After a TREMENDOUS amount of bullshit,. I found out this line was a fraud,. (wait,. really?).They folded,. and I got one check.It was a good one though,. about $1,000.I had to wait a month to get paid,which drove me nuts as I was broke at the time.

Broke again,. (couldn't I see this coming?),. I started to look for a FOURTH line,and got the job hooked up,when my life circumstance changed again,sending me to my currant location:My $125 a week rented room in Washington Heights NYC,. the Dominican Republic stronghold.

Turned out the psychic biz just wasn't for me,. and now I folded.I would eventually find my next survival system,. walking and washing Dogs.

I enjoyed our happy,quiet,walks.An occasional BARK,. was more welcome than,.

"Will he leave his wife and kids to be with me?"

Anyway,. some publisher out dere' want to pay for full disclosure? Hit me up.

Whenever I try to examine this part of my life,It gets blurry.I walked off my own path in an act of desperation,seeking truth.My own truth.It shouldn't take a whole lifetime to understand what some people are born knowing.A few days after I quit this job for what I hope was the last time,. my spirit guide asked me . . .

"So,. what did you LEARN?"

BEYOND DRAMA 6

Like millions of people I have experienced the Joy of surgery.Some folks have no doubt had WAY worse experiences than me.Still,. there is something special in being rendered completely,utterly,and totally,. helpless and powerless.The body always wins in the end.We need our body more than anything,. yet we do so much to destroy it.In three separate occasions in my life I have had to either have surgery or lose to the ability to walk,. and finally to LIVE.

Throughout my childhood I had a problem with my knees . . .

They would DISLOCATE.

DISLOCATION is fun.You fall down and cant do anything until your knee is RElocated,. put back in place.This may not happen right away,and you'll spend time wondering if you'll ever get it back in,. its traumatizing to say the least.I POPPED my knees back in many times,. and I was usually quite upset.I wouldn't be able to walk for several days.It started mostly in Little League,. where I was an all-star catcher by the way,. with my batting average on my wall.I was a kid . . . and running around was required.BAM!! Over and over it would happen.

At first the doctors prescribed KNEE BRACES,. no different than like Forest freaking Gump.RUN FOREST,RUN.These devices humiliated me and turned me into a robocop wanna-be.Worse,. they didn't work.my knees got worse and worse and until I literally couldn't walk.

So at 15,. my right knee was done. They unhooked and shortened my hamstring and did knot tying and some crazy shit. After 5 hours I was in a huge cast. Not the first time,. as I had been hit by a car when I was 13,. a secret chapter of the FAT DRAMA,. where being fat saved my life. I split my left arm,. the upper arm,. in half that day,. chasing a ball in the street. The car was going about 30mph and I destroyed the radiator. I was knocked out and my brother threatening the driver was the last thing I remember. I was brought back by a REALLY fat guy with a heart of gold,. a volunteer fireman that was across the street. That Firehouse siren that sounded, and sounds every day at noon, stays with me till today.

After the right knee was done,. I knew the left knee might not last,. but it seemed ok . . .

So,. Aries style,. In my high school marching band, I tried to play football with the actual football team,. and refused to go down when I was tackled by 3 or 4 guys. POP!

Then I woke up one day and went from bed to basketball and tried to do some fantasy Michael Jordan shit. POP! I'll never forget laying in the street unable to move and just quietly listening to the morning birds sing about how much they Love the Sun. My father found me out there about an hour later.

Next,. I was sitting on the toilet taking a shit. POP!

That was it,. and now I couldn't walk again. Surgery time . . . except this time I had no insurance coverage. I signed something saying I would pay. Naked and blind on the table I was awake and the surgeon played my Duke Ellington cd that he said I could bring. The cd started to skip.

"TURN THAT SHIT OFF!",. was the last thing I remember,. and I woke up in a cast. That night I reached my maximum dose of pain killers right away,. but it was only 1am.

I SCREAMED AND BEGGED ALL NIGHT.

The nurses were rough,. and my SLEEP APNEA Didn't help.I survived only to find I was $60,000 in debt at 18.POP! There was my FIRST Bankruptcy.

FAST FORWARD.

I'm on stage in Brooklyn playing Jazz trumpet and Bass Clarinet on a live radio show with my good friend Matthew Heyner,. on bass.The music is great,. but I'm SWEATING.Don't know why.

Suddenly A KNIFE TWISTS IN MY SIDE.

AHHHHHGGHHHHH!! WTF?!

Whatever it was went away,until a few minutes later,.

AGGGHHHHH!!!!!! WTF?! Started that NBA sweat . . .

An invisible knife tWiStEd aNd tURNEd . . .

Must be GAS,. right? I made it home and drank a gallon of Pepto Bismol and stared at my Christmas lights,. it was also my fathers birthday.I wasn't sleeping,. it was 5am.

AGGGGHHHHHHHHH!

I called a car and checked myself into a hospital.As soon as they saw me,. I was taken to X-ray.At X-ray I waited in a flimsy hospital gown,. (my keys,wallet,and glasses were gone),while a man who was in a horrible car accident was looked at.Someone mumbled "he may have broken every bone in his body."AGGGGHH!!!!

People in hospitals are desensitised,. as my cries of pain were left on deaf ears.A nurse asked me to again sign something saying I would pay,. and then a doctor explained that my

Appendix was minutes from going POP,. and if it did,. I could DIE. I overheard nurses talking about some bullshit from the comedy Friends on TV,. and for some reason I was in the area for people with Heart problems. The nurse yelled at me for having my gown open when she saw my balls. I was delirious.

Next memory,. a COLD table and a BRIGHT Light. The table is shaped like the crucifix so they can put all these needles in my arm. I'm thinking how all the woman nurses are seeing my disgusting fat belly wondering how to CUT through to SEIZE my appendix. Was this an alien abduction? Did they have the PROBE?

Next memory: I wake up in ICU.

"WHAT ARE YOU DOING? YOU SHOULD BE ASLEEP!!"

(I couldn't move an inch) …"Someday I'm going to visit the islands,. or California,. can you come with me?" (to the nurse)

Next memory: An older Indian woman is waking me up with a wire snake,. the CATHETER. She explains that she has to use this plumbing device, AND PUT IT UP INSIDE MY PENIS.

FUCK NO!! GET OFF OF ME!! THERE MUST BE ANOTHER OPTION!!

. . .

There wasn't.

. . .

I spent a week with my MOM after that trying to recover. It was brutal. I went back to work earlier than I should,. no vacation time left,. and passed out several times trying to process the Tower records return for the month,. around $350,000 I recall. My boss tried to send me home,. but I was the only one that knew how to process it.

Now I'm 41 ... 1 out of 15 people catch the ol' Appendix mendix. I don't miss surgery,. but can only imagine as I get older what may be in store for me next.

S'ok, ... I'm used to it by now.

. . .

I think.

BEYOND DRAMA 7

What's it like to never sleep?

God made the Sun.God made the Earth.God made the Moon.God made the human body. God made SLEEP.We MUST sleep or die.

"Sleep . . . those little slices of death,. how I loathe them . . .",. one of my favorite quotes,. I forget from who.

SLEEP APNEA is very common in America since we went wrong and don't take care of ourselves worse than any culture on Earth.In my case,. besides being out of shape,. I have an "unusually narrow wind passage",. strange for a trumpet player who likes to BLOW.

It started in High school.Bizarre EXTREME snoring,. or what people assume is snoring. The reality? I stop breathing when I sleep,. and then my body FORCES me to breathe.This creates a constant back and forth by the body to attempt sleep,and then wake itself to survive,. escaping death by mere inches.This evil dance lasts all night long as you become a prisoner of your own body.

What happens is you never really sleep,. and never establish that RHYTHM that is so vital,. when the body TEMPO slows down so the heart,more than anything,can rest.Besides freaking out anyone nearby,. sleep apnea means you will never have a complete dream,. and after awhile,. your life becomes a nightmare.People that heard my body forcing me to breathe while my soul is trying to travel say it's a quite frightening,. and of course destroys the sleep of anyone nearby.It's VERY Loud,. and beyond description really.Great for relationships.

Walking around like this for YEARS almost drove me mad,. and I almost lost my sanity to be honest.

FLASHBACK:

I'm living in Nyack NY on main street and working the night shift,. (see previous drama),. and not only do I have sleep apnea,. but now I'm trying to IMPROVISE a sleep pattern during the day.

WHEN THE SUN IS OUT YOU MIGHT NAP, BUT YOU DON'T SLEEP

So I'm "S l E e Pi N g gg one day,. when I wake up to someone rubbing my back. I feel it,. and then a voice in my ear says,. "Heeey ..." in a gentle way. Someone is sitting next to me,. I feel the weight on my bed.

Hmmm, ... but nobody is home but me,. and the door is locked.

I'M BEING TOUCHED BY A GHOST?!

I FREAKED,. took my blanket and went across the street to a Pizza parlor during lunch and wouldn't go back in. When they threatened to call the mental police,. I went back inside,. but NOT to sleep.

The problem was,. I still think it was a REAL experience.

But, ... it was enough to seek help. I ended up at a sleep disorder clinic and they covered my head with wires like Frankenstein and filmed me "sleeping",. to tell me that I woke up 278 times the first night and 324 the next. The prescription was the famous CPAP machine,. an O2 machine with a mask that you wear to bed that forces you to breathe all night. The problem is the mask comes off,. or you just get so tired of sleeping on your back,. you don't care.

BUT IF YOU DON'T SLEEP WITH THE MASK YOU MIGHT DIE!!

Fair enough.I still don't know how I did it,. but by eating better,and a great deal of exercise,. I somehow taught my body to control my condition to a degree.It got bad again,. and I had another sleep study at Columbia University,. but when they said CPAP again,. I just somehow forced myself well.As of late,. I'm not eating as good as I should,. but somehow the condition receded,. like my hairline . . . never to return.CPAP was a great relationship tool,. I should tell Dr.Phil bout' that shit.

During the bad period I would catch insomnia or just be freaking out over ghosts and just losing my mind in general.One summer the Insomnia was so bad,. I knew I was dying,. I could actually feel and taste death,. walking around Queens like a Zombie praying for help.I used to work and try to be a Jazz musician at night during these periods,. and work might be unloading trucks all day.I went to acupuncture quite often seeking a natural cure.

Someone,. some force,. pulled me up from this sleep ocean that I was drowning in.Was it astrology I wondered? It felt like I was up against what I call Natural forces.Were the planets doing this to me? Kind of like sexual desire,. there seems to be no escape,. as the natural forces rise like the TIDE.

Thank God I found still water,. peaceful as the glass pond at 4am in China,. to live and Breathe again . . .

And now dear reader,. we go beyond the beyond into the best of my blog writing.I truly appreciate the time you have spent with me.The following is how I developed a small online audience as I search not for the meaning of life,but the meaning in it.By and large JAZZ is at the center of most of the following songs.I write the same way I play music,the same way I talk.The same way I live.

THE NIGHT JAZZ BECAME ITSELF

A few months ago,. Giuseppi Logan called me up and said,. "man,. we have to work,. I can't get any work,. I'm broke man." Giuseppi is under the impression that we can make enough money playing music to have our rent paid,and and enough food in our stomachs so that they stop growling at us.I had exhausted all my limited options,. and now started to understand that Brother G has just not been received back even close to how brother Grimes was a few years ago.Giuseppi has never been stronger in the time that I've known him,. and we've had some BRIGHT moments,. notably in Philly,. when Dave Burrell came by and we just BURNED the ARS nova arts center to the ground.We opened the ESP Albert Ayler festival about a month ago,. which was also great.G's CD has actually just sold out.

BUT,. that hasn't changed the fact that he has just about no money to live on on a daily basis and has become so much a part of Tompkins square Park in NYC,. that if he wasn't there playing during the day,. the park might not even EXIST.Still,. we refuse to just let it go,. . . after all,. music is all we have.The 35 years between us don't amount to a hill of beans next to our mutual addiction to music.Play the music we live or die.Being down and wasn't going to stop us.Not this time.

So I reached out again to folks that might be able to send G some LOVE,. and brother John Zorn responded,. literally in about 5 minutes from my email,. saying he was taking action,. knew Giuseppi,. and had heard him in the park.A very short time after that,. Brother G had a gig booked at the STONE.Maybe the number one spot in NYC for the music we love.

Our usual crew was out of town so we called up G's personal friend,drummer Gerard Faroux,. a sweet cat that can swing.Another brother G,. Gerard grew up in France.He's just about the same age as Giuseppi.He was subbing for drum legend Warren Smith.My long term brother Francois Grillot was actually in France,. so we reached out to one of the greatest and favorite bass players in NYC,. brother Hilliard Greene.The stage was set for our concert,. last night,. a 10pm Sunday set.

I had to take a cab from the West side,. after a concert with my great friend Ras Moshe,. and asked the driver to drive up Giuseppe's block.Sure enough,. there was G and his alto boppin up the street,. in a suit and sneakers,. and his wild white beard.I asked the cab to pull over and got G to jump in."Hey man, . . . where's this Stone at?"

9:59:There's about 4 people in the audience,. but G and I are amped up anyway,. ready to play,. to REALLY play,. and he's playing piano for himself as a few people watch,. not sure what's happening,. and then . . .

BOOM! The place is packed,. and people have that eager anticipation thing going, . . . somehow just knowing there about to experience something special.I myself was tired from really going for it on the show bout an hour before,. but as soon as I saw Hill next to me ready to go,. I felt like Lee Morgan himself was the front row.

"Show me what you got."

Then,. it just HAPPENED . . .

Giuseppi started into his tune BOP DUES.Everyone thinks of him from his records as the mystery OUT cat,. and he IS that guy,. but he also wants to just PLAY, . . . the best he possibly can,. and once we escape his crisp little swinging bop line,. we just start bReAkInG iT DoWn.SwIrLiNg and tWiRLInG.I came out and did some WhirLInG.Hill chose to BOB n WeAvE,. while Gerard did the crisp BRisK n' wHisk.

3 different generations,. both In and Out,. free,. and swinging,. all there TOGETHER,. trying to just BE together.Somehow Jazz,. whatever it's supposed to be,. BECAME,. and a slight clue as to what she really is was revealed.Wasn't about the right changes or the most complicated heads.It was about our SOUNDS,. and the stories of our lives.It was freedom of expression above all.Sing your song where you FEEL it, . . . play the sound of your life.

People may not know what they were being a part of,. but they FELT they were and started yelling to us in support and also letting themselves be a part of us being together. They were now part of US and we were ALL together. I thought about Charles Mingus,. and just why we play. It doesn't happen that often,. but every now and then the music reminds us that what we are really does mean something important,. something special.

It means,. that were alive.

Giuseppi wasn't done,. not by a long shot,... as we got into "Under My Skin",. "Cherokee",. "Over the Rainbow",. and more,. all G style,. which had everybody dancing in their skin. Giuseppi finished every one off with his vocal from record,. "Love me tonight",. as he told me,. "I Want them to Love me!,. I want the people to Love me!" Afterwords a dear friend of mine came to me with tears in her eyes and said,. "Bless you". Well,. all of us our blessed with the ability to actually be who we are every now and then. Giuseppi helped show me that to in his own G way.

"We can play man! We can play!"

See,. it could be that in that end,... all Jazz really is,. is a 4 letter word ... for Love ...

Grandpas rainbow

Just how and why does anybody dedicate their lives to Art in a fallen world? To make such a choice in 2010 would be over the top from my perspective. When I was a kid in the 70's I had no idea that the gentrification express was all ready rolling along and that standards had all ready begun to fall across the board as to what was actually important and held meaning in every aspect of life. I remember being in my mom's pine green Volkswagen bug,. engine in the back,. trunk in the front, waiting in line for Gas for 2 hours when the gas station guy put a sign on the car in front of us that said NO MORE GAS. I had no idea that the foundation of who I was and who I was going to be was all ready being built by in large by my relationship with my Grandfather,. Fritz. My grandfather is THE reason I am who I am today.

Fritz . . . man,. he was really something. My grandfather was a great painter and sculptor. You know the statue at the skating rink in Rockefeller center in NYC? My grandfather's job was to keep it GOLD. His day gig was restoring art,. and he worked on everything at Rockefeller center,. a MAJOR gig. After work he worked on his own art which ranged from portraits to sculptured busts to even working on the living stations for his church. (The living stations are small sculptures, each depicting another stage of Jesus on his way to crucifixion and eventual Resurrection.) From his perspective,. there was no other way to see his work as other than being a gift from God. His portraits,. large acrylic paintings,. had a special quality about them,. capturing what it was like to actually be around the person being painted. My prized possessions are his two busts: Martin Luther King Jr,. and Beethoven. They are SO real,. so human. Absolutely incredible work. He only did a few shows of his own work when I knew him,. one time because my Mother insisted upon it and really helped make it happen. I would pursue Art as my creative outlet up to my second year of college when Jazz finally took over once and for all. (I hope to return to painting someday,. like Miles did.). One day I showed him my drawing of the planets in our Solar System. It was pretty weak,. but I remember him encouraging me to keep working on it.(what he would also say after beating me in Chess). I'll also never forget watching his sculptures cook in his KILN.Incredible.

How did this relate to a 8-11 year old kid?

My Grandfather invited me into his world at this young age and let me be a part of it.Direct access to his inner world of creation.Something I cherish and will never forget.While I never was able to co-create with him,. he showed me the things in life behind his art,. what was important to him,and why he was an artist.For him,. the creation of art was a spiritual task,. which led to his relationship with God:My grandfather was a devout Catholic.He was in fact the artist on staff at the church which he worked tirelessly for for free.I will never forget seeing the priest,. Father Rooney,openly crying at his wake.Seeing a priest touched so strongly by my grandfather's life had enormous impact on me to say the least.

As a kid he was THE example of who to be,. so I tried to be the best grandson I could,. going to church with him every day,. sitting in the front row,and praying as LOUD as I could.(My Mother also has a history of getting loud in church to this day).One time the sermon was ABOUT me,. the kid in the front row who was more into church than all the adults in the room,. which made my grandfather very proud.Back at home my Grandfather would spontaneously have the desire to say the Rosary and then he would haul my brother and I off the street from playing inside to pray with him.I'll never forget the passion with which he did this.More than anything,. I'll never forget his daily "List",. a piece of paper with all the people and things that we needed to pray for that day.After my Grandfather passed away my relationship with Catholicism faded away,. but the impact of sharing that experience with him was forever.(My two weeks as an Altar boy didn't work out)

Going deeper,. the greatest connection my Grandfather gave me however was one that neither one of us could see at the time,. the one to MUSIC.One of his favorite things to do on his downtime was to sit in a room with the lights turned down and listen to classical symphonies.Long ones. Eventually he started not just inviting me to these listening sessions,. but just telling me,. "Now we are going to listen to the gift of music".Some of these listening sessions lasted 2 to 4 hours and as a kid,. I had a hard time getting into the music.The deep impact was made by me sitting there watching how much this music meant to him,. I could see the emotion in his face. We never spoke of the music as all he would gently say was "Listen".

"Listen."

I left those listening sessions knowing that music was important. Now I just had to wait for music to find me and show me which way to go. I played trumpet in 4th grade and was always praised for my exuberance. It wasn't until High School when legendary music educator Bert Hughes found me though,. that my course was charted. In Jazz band one day,. Bert played the Basie band playing "Splanky". "Just listen", he told the class.

"Listen."

Back in the early 80's,. time went on, my parents divorced, (Divorce was not as popular then as it is now),. and my Grandfather was diagnosed with Liver Cancer. My Grandmother had all ready been suffering from bad Parkinson's disease and couldn't walk for several years. My final memories of my Grandfather are him leaving his death bed to help his wife walk to the bathroom,. and him calling me to his side the night before he died to explain that it was time for him to return home,. and that I was now the man of the house. (I was only 12 and far from being capable of that kind of responsibility but I told him I accepted this.)

As my Mother drove my Brother and I to my Grandfather's Funeral a couple days later,. We came upon the biggest and brightest Rainbow I have ever seen. With tear's in her eyes,. my Mother turned to my Brother and I in the back seat and said:

"There it is Boys,. Do you See it?"

"Grandpa's Rainbow"

Music from the future

I often refer to the Spiritual side of Jazz and in particular,. free Jazz,. no less than like a preacher on the pulpit.Some folks consider a spiritual perspective on music an excuse to just play wild and free with no real focus and or maybe no real skill.How much skill do you need to engage any music from a spiritual perspective? Which music is closer to God,. John Coltrane's Interstellar Space or somebody singing Amazing Grace down at the Church? I feel that the better I can reach my own ideas,. the more prepared I am for when the BIG feelings come,. regardless of how spiritual they may or may not be.I have watched my own music vary in very close relationship to how I'm FEELING at the time,. all though I sometimes have to check all that THINKING at the door.Jazz in 2010 is a real trip in that we actually have a few scientists,. and maybe even a few,. very few, ...

Spiritualists

Having recently seen the movie <u>CONTACT</u>,. staring Jodie Foster,. I was struck by the war between science and religion through the whole film,.

I recently said to drummer Marc Edwards on Facebook of all places, . . . that the same portal Jodie went through,. is the one we open when we play music.(He agreed).The film touches on a very real conflict in perspective in 2 very different takes on what reality actually is.Religion and Science dominate a vast amount of people in the World as an effort to make sense of this reality and enable them to function.Religion uses fear and science uses the mind,. (to possibly attempt to control fear of the unknown),. holding up evidence as something holy.Of course,Governments get in between the 2 and make everything even worse trying to structure and control the people.What does this have to do with Jazz musicians?

I'll go out on a limb and suggest that 2 of the greatest Jazz musicians of all time SOLVED the conflict that most of the world wrestles with today,by combining the best of both the Science and Religious worlds,while leaving behind the worst.One thing great Jazz musicians all have in common is that they are not AFRAID.John Coltrane and Ornette Coleman were not afraid to confront reality itself with their music.They in fact challenged the reality of music itself at the time that they began their journey's into their own musical worlds,. because they seemingly had no other choice. They simply HAD to do what they did.

Check out Dr.Lewis Porter's transcriptions of Coltrane's work on Interstellar Space.Was Trane a scientist? No,. but his mastery of harmony and technical ability reached a level that was,.

Profound.

A technical take on what Trane was doing would reveal an immensely personal language he spent years creating and had developed an almost impossible technique to achieve.He was doing things with sound,and utilizing harmony in such a way,. that it could,. to me,. be looked on no differently,. from a technical perspective,. than looking at the work of someone trying to CURE CANCER.He has to be the most advanced Jazz musician of all time in regards to harmony.

But Coltrane was not playing to reach the apex of technical,or scientific discovery,. he was trying to find a way deeper and deeper into the reality of himself,. and the reality of the reality that there are things in life beyond what we can see with our physical eyes,. and things we can only see with our soul eyes.I'm not a member of the Church that ordained him,. and I don't elevate him to being ABOVE us.Rather,. I believe that his journey shows that higher aspects of reality all ready exist in all of us.Maybe WE are God,. as some have suggested.

By taking his music to both technical (How I equate science into the equation),and spiritual extremes,. he was able to go WAY past what he would have been able to find had he chosen one,closed perspective.Was his journey worth it? Depends how open you are,. how afraid you are,and how willing you are to allow access into both those sides of yourself in order to evolve in both ways,. as a body and as a soul.Both perspectives call for a great deal of WORK.(Cue:the MONK song)

Ornette Coleman has a degree in Chemistry.As we all know,. he created a philosophy that changed Jazz forever called Harmelodics,. which has a PARTIALLY SCIENTIFIC FOUNDATION.There is big time music theory behind Harmelodics,. and OC will tell you he has mastered the world of chords,having spent his life researching them.In the same breath,. OC will tell you,.

"The Soul is Eternal" ...

A scientist might say that is something we tell ourselves so that we fear death a little less.A religion person might say that is a law of God.Ornette's gifts to the world have basis in both Science and a spirituality that may have some roots in the church.We are all better for it by stepping outside category,. and just being,. just playing.Duke himself always spoke of reaching beyond categories

Where is Trane now? Continuing his search? Look me up on the personal for further discussion here,. as some parts of life I'm only willing to speak about in person.What will music sound like in 5555? (anybody want to meet me there?)

I'm not against Science or religion if it indeed allows people to function in this world.If folks need it to focus on so that they can get out of bed in the morning,. so be it.For a scientist,. science is his music,. and for the religious folks,. religion may be there music.The trouble is all those LAWS and RULES both camps haul all over creation.Jazz musicians tend to BREAK rules,. don't we? I would suggest that human beings created JAZZ,. not God,. all though I cant prove it.Anyway,.

Religions all over the Earth have accepted God in some fashion as the basis of their existence,. the power of Faith.

Scientists want proof that God exists.They want someone to prove God exists.What if someone DID prove it to them?

Matt Lavelle

John Coltrane,.

Almost . . .

Did just.that.

For VEGA!

The Unison

I'm not an expert on Alice Coltrane and her music,. but I do know that her music has reached out to me in the last few years,and acted as a guide in some way about how to process the relationship of spirit to music.Her music after Trane made the transition fascinates me,and I intend to listen to all of it at some point.That's the kind of box set we need these days if you ask me.Musing on the relationship I have formed with her music opens up a whole other door about the way men and woman relate to music differently. This to,. is something I'm not an expert on,. and some would argue that there is no difference in the way men and woman relate to music,. that were both human beings so there really are no differences.This is what led to one of my assignments,given to me by Ornette Coleman,. in an attempt to further understand this spiritual musical relationship inside myself,and also to broaden the sense of my relationship to the world,. and also to see just how incredible it is that the creator can cause SO much to happen with one simple act, . . . seperate us as men and woman.

"Form a band comprised of all woman,. play some concerts,. and then report back and tell me what you've learned".

At least half of the time I have spent talking to OC has not been not about music,. but about woman,and what happens when we get together.He speaks of them in a reverential tone,. with him usually ending by speaking about his mother.("I know who you are",. she would have to tell the young Ornette over and over).Deep love and respect for our mother's is common ground for us.Woman seem to simply gravitate closer to their emotional center,for better or for worse,. and emotional expression is another thing both OC and myself believe to be paramount.Ornette is really something in that his intellectual process IS emotional,. more than any other musician I've played with,. and it's really a super-natural type of experience. The emotional search for new ideas is something that happens to him in real time,. and since he FEELS so strongly about ideas,. his Pieces sensitivity thing is just played out to the extreme. His dynamic sensitivity has really gotten to me more than anything: whispering in somebody's ear has a lot more impact at times than shouting in their face,. (although we all need to get our shout on now and then.)

Back to ALICE. I really believe she extended her husbands music and used it as a template to explore even further down the path that Trane had to follow at a higher vibration. I believe they stayed in contact,. bonded on another level through music and creating a family together. What if they never got together? What would Alice's music be like then? What if Trane never met Miles? Fact is that some relationships are just meant to be as part of that master plan I'd say. I never got to meet and talk with Alice,. a major regret. Her return to music a year before her own transition has me shook. As spiritual as she was,. was she aware that her transition was coming and that her and her music had to say goodbye to the world as we know it? When you go as deep as she did in music and spirituality,. I believe that level of access to life is possible. I've had experiences with powerful spiritual people that defy explanation,. since they are no longer with us.

Or are they?

Listening to Alice's song,. Journey in Satchidananda,. hundred's of times,. led me to play the song in every key and direction during a music event with Charles Downs, (myself on trumpet), that had me so open that my own Sun in the third house was given a chance to be itself,. and Alice started talking to me right there,. as Charles took over on drums,. like a big WAVE washing over me. Playing her music with as much intent as I was reached out and called to her across the space-ways.

"I LIKE you Matt . . . I have followed your musical journey,. and I'm here to tell you to KEEP. GOING. You Have something to say! Your contribution is VITAL,. and no matter what you do,. keep playing. You need it. We need it. The World needs it."

Then on a concert with Eric Mingus,. I felt a HUGE presence standing next to me during the music,. right after I played a solo where I tried to be as BLUE as possible.I heard a voice.Loud,. passionate,. almost angry:

"Believe this! If we were alive at the same time,. you would be in MY band! . . ."

I said nothing,. but thought to myself,.., that might really be the best place for me.If only.I think I might have just FIT in that environment.Could it be that playing Bass Clarinet with his son,. with THAT much intent,. reached out to him as well? These experiences were very real.

Back to Alice again, . . . and I need to study her life,. and especially the choices she made and when she made them.Coming through the house that Trane built,. she would go on to build her own house,. and then even a church in a sense.(A literal Ashram).Sometimes Blues just POURED out of her,. and that ORGAN!! She sounded like Trane sometimes with that.Then the HARP!! Alice really just opened everything up with the harp,. just WEAVING INTRICATE INFINITE tapestries of sound.Her Harp music might be from the year 5555. (Oh yeah,. wait,. time's a CIRCLE).I take one of Alice's messages to be to EMBRACE the spiritual power in music,. not run from it,. and to not let your own fear get in the way. Could Trane have done anything he did if he was AFRAID of himself? Alice's music has many signposts she left us as she blazed that trail.I'm ready to listen.BEEN ready.

The greatest musical experience of my life up to this point is a duo with OC where I brought over an alto Clarinet,. and we ended up in the way upper register of the alto's playing the same notes,. holding them out,. over and over again,. pouring our hearts out together.

Afterwords Ornette said, . . .

"There it was,. maybe the greatest thing there is in music, . . . and in life" . . .

"The Unison"

Sacred music sex with the WIND

Sometimes my worlds come together.

Even NYC feels the change of the seasons at times. We actually had tornadoes touch down in Queens and Brooklyn recently, ripping up and throwing trees around,. causing electrical mayhem. The last few days I've been in wind gusts blowing new yorkers right into traffic. (Hold on to a mailbox if it gets really bad). I live way uptown not far from the river and the wind is especially strong the closer you get to the water. Sometimes the wind has to travel through the streets broken up by all the buildings,. and you end up in an actual wind tunnel. Chicago and Boston have this happening big time.

Way down in Brooklyn they have far less high rise buildings,. and I was out in the warehouse district where you can actually see the sky. (Gentrification will change this soon enough). The clouds had a really fast tempo,. just MOVING. They looked lower and stretched out. I knew the wind was behind this. I was in Brooklyn to perform music for the festival of new trumpet music organization and just had my flugelhorn. I arrived early and felt the urge to play outside and "activate my lip", . . . a brass thing.

My flugelhorn,. also known as HOT SILVER,. is really something. She has a whole story and history like all horns,. but she has stayed with me as the others have come and gone. I'll never leave her as long as she decides to stay. I've had her for over 20 years, and got her with a credit card that I declared bankruptcy on. She's a Yamaha lightweight model,. which I didn't know when we first got together. She's been on life support at times and was once saved from meltdown by my man Josh Landress,. brass master.

The Flugelhorn is a fat wide open horn with a tinge of sweetness. Flesh on metal is the actual physical relationship that turns her on,. a true WIND instrument. It's taken me years to understand her unique sound production and potential,. and how you cant be rough on her like you can a trumpet. You can get rough on a trumpet and she'll give you attitude,. but try to get rough on a flugel and she will take away her SOUND. She just leaves unless you take your time. (Roy Campbell Jr revealed some of the secrets of this craft to me.) It's taken me many years of searching to discover and accept that she reveals my most personal voice.

Not only that, . . . but she lets me talk to the WIND . . .

As I started to play long tones outside on that deserted Brooklyn street corner,. I felt an instant connection to the natural energy outside. The Sun had set about 3 hours earlier. As I played I suddenly felt an actual physical and spiritual connection to the wind,. stronger than I feel on my usual riverbank music meditations. The longer I played,. the stronger the connection felt,. until I felt gusts coming right down the street and sweeping all around me.

The wind wanted to PLAY. She was asking me to send her right through the horn,. so we could let the Earth sing her song. I felt like I was a tree,. with my roots reaching down into the center of the Earth while my top branches could reach high up in the sky and feel the wind that only the birds get to enjoy.

I just let it happen. We bonded,. and I let her sing an ancient,. yet present,. and future song all at once. As she sang her song I understood that the Wind has been here on Earth since the very beginning. She has seen civilizations rise and fall,. and that we may be no different. We come and go,. but she has ALWAYS been here. We never listen,. but I was doing more than listening now. For this brief moment in time,. she was letting me BE her. I also was allowed to feel the true nature of her power.

That's when I received a simple message,. as clear as the sweetest sound you'll ever hear.

"Earth changes are coming.Major changes on the scale that nobody on Earth has ever experienced.Your not ready."

"It has NEVER been more important for the artist to paint,. the musician to play,. the writer to write,. and the sculptor to sculpt.The art that humanity creates is the only reason your still allowed to exist.The Earth has no choice but to be herself,. DESPITE the human race. She will regain her balance no matter the cost"

"When you play music,. you can join with nature on much deeper levels than you do now. Access this power to help with the transformation of all that is."

I then found myself in a place of total stillness,calm and peace.Like a lake at 4am.Not a single ripple or sound.

Total Silence.

She left me.Moved on.I was all alone.

My flugelhorn was still in my hand though.

I went inside to play,. and knew what had to happen next . . .

Dedicated to the Wind, and every Flugelhorn on Earth

CLIFFORD BROWN . . . THE COMET.

Hearing the opening of the Clifford Brown birthday broadcast on WKCR at midnight this past Saturday,a 30 hour marathon,got me to reflect again on what I call the trumpet brotherhood,. and Clifford Brown's towering place inside of it.In 2010 it's hard to find members of the brotherhood,. but we still exist.Of course We all start with Louis Armstrong who passed on when I was four years old.You can really chart the progression of the Trumpet in Jazz through members of the brotherhood.Clifford Brown was no different than a COMET who quickly passed through to display what we could be,and then moved on to a place of higher vibration that some of us try to reach when we engage the horn. Clifford was saying of course that we can be Comets ourselves,. not knowing that people would be learning his solos for years and years as an attempted stairway to the stars.

The first time I saw JOY SPRING on paper I was presented with a mountain I didn't even have a map to find,. much less climb.I couldn't even play the melody much less that graceful D# above the staff that he uses in such a beautiful lyrical way.Just by looking at the notes on paper I learned that you don't have to go Maynard when you go upstairs.Lee Morgan,. who was great friends with Clifford,. reinforced this with another tune that kicked my ass for years,. CEORA.These kind of tunes have always found me over the years,. tunes that reveal your weaknesses or strengths.Playing the changes to GROOVIN' HIGH always bugged me out.(Ornette freed me from this drama,. but presented me with bigger problems that were more important and difficult to solve).

Right in those songs however,. you can see connections inside the Jazz trumpet brotherhood,. or what I also call the great TREE.Many of us see the Tree in different ways.I used to argue with my friend,and great trumpet player,Gilbert Castellanos that FATS came right out of DIZZY,. and he insisted that it was Dizzy that came from Fats.I'm still not sure who influenced who more,. but I do know they both had simply incredible conceptions and original sounds that make most players today little branches all the way at the top of the tree,. which can only grow so far right? (heh)

Many agree that Fats was a big influence on Clifford,. although it's always been hard for me to see since I gravitate towards Clifford so much more,by way of Lee,Booker Little,Thad Jones,Nat Adderley,Woody Shaw,Freddie Hubbard,Hannibal,Donald Ayler,Don Cherry,Raphe,and Roy Campbell Jr.I've never been into Donald Byrd,. who to me always sounds like a branch on the Clifford tree.What bugs me out is that Clifford was playing so much incredible music at such a young age.My favorite Lee Morgan is when he was not yet TWENTY.What is it about firing off these lines at that time of your life? It was a different time for sure,. but I'm always trying to find that EXUBERANCE,. even if I've been working all day(Some times a large Bodega Coffee helps,. but that's all I do).I'm 40 and have all ready out lived Clifford,Fats,Booker,Lee,Bird,and Eric Dolphy.I've often mused that they played their life's music while they were here.They all have recorded musical legacies standing the test of time many years later.

Clifford again,. didn't need no SMACK to elevate.His music is so Human.I hear the struggle,. the honesty,. the Holy Blues.(My strength).Clifford had everything so many can't find today in this fallen world.(Props to Larry Roland for using his way of describing today's environment).I aspire to reach the highest levels of expression that Clifford Brown reached for every time he played,. seemingly without an ounce of FEAR.The first time I met Sonny Rollins I had nothing to say on trumpet,. but I knew I could ask him about Clifford who was an inspiration to find a voice.I'll never forget his EMOTIONAL reaction when I asked him about Clifford Brown not as a musician,. but as a human being.Sonny Rollins told me that Clifford was an example of the payoff of HARD WORK.Sonny said that Clifford's dedication to practice and getting better every day was a genuine and real path to reach the top of the mountain.I've seen this level of dedication in the masters,. something they never relinquish.I once played with Ornette for 8 hours straight,. and he was playing

FULL BORE. I understand that Sonny still plays 5 hours a day. I've never accepted weekend warrior status myself and will work on music at least 2 hours a day no matter how many hours I worked that day.

Translation: No rest,. this is LIFE. You never know when your done,. just ask Clifford.

I read that at Louis Armstrong's memorial or funeral,. maybe even before he passed,. that Dizzy Gillespie said of Louis,: "No YOU,. no ME" . . .

As a trumpet player in 2010,. I can't separate myself from the great tree before me. I can just try to be my own branch. Some folks are planting new tree's which I can respect. How do you plant a tree with no seeds though? What if the soil is messed up and you cant TAKE ROOT? Some folks smoke trees. Even if I planted my own, . . . MILES would stop by and ask me what I was doing that for.

"Hey Miles,. you need a Bass Clarinet?"

Happy Birthday Clifford. Sorry you left so soon. Your LIGHT is still burning BRIGHT. One of the TRUE Kings. You and Max together again! Can you send some Love to 2010?

Peace.

Me,Diz,and that Coffee cup

Just what happens to people when they enter the personal space of people who are doing something at the highest levels,. Cultural Icons? Hero worship is a real Problem in Jazz and Free jazz today,. and coming up,. I was especially vulnerable . . .

First one was when I was about 17 and went backstage to meet Wynton Marsalis, . . . scared as a motherfucker,. having heard him play trumpet REALLY well,. when I had about 22% of my style and sound together. During the show I yelled out TAIN!,. during a quiet moment,. which made the whole audience,. at a big hall in Tarrytown NY,. do a double take.(this was an actual shout out to the drummer Jeff tain Watts,. as I was caught up in the moment).Back stage was a family vibe and I approached Wynton and waited until the group of people around him parted,. like the great Red Sea.I was tripping,. and Wynton looked at me,. shook my hand and said,. "I'm not gonna HIT you man",. Wynton was cool though! Very supportive,. and I would cross paths with him several more times . . . (to be continued) . . .

Next one I regretted for years, . . . KING Sonny Rollins.Backstage after a concert in New Paltz New york.There was a small group hanging with Sonny,. and he was being really cool about it.A friend of mine gave him a bunch of Roses and started crying,. But Sonny was cool about that to,. a Deep human being.

Then I came out and said, . . .

"Who was taller?,.You or Coltrane?", . . .

DAMN, . . . that was weak, . but Sonny was STILL cool, . and said about 6, . . . 6-1, . and showed me about where the top of his head was. For years that haunted me, . and I thought about having to stay cool, . and having SOME INTELLIGENT SHIT TO SAY . . . Just a few years ago, . I rectified this with SR, . when I got to be his assistant at an IAJE autograph signing, . But I still almost Fucked up again!, . . . "What's my favorite Sonny Rollins solo I asked?", . Sonny was like, .?, . then I said, ."3 Little Words", . from Sonny On impulse . . . He stopped, . and lowered his shades, . and made eye contact with me, . . .

"Me to man, . . . me to"

I felt about 9 miles high, . . . (whew, . what a relief) . . .

This, . and my encounter with DIZ, . was all in preparation for 2 years of studying with OC. I would end up 1 on 1 with OC in his House straight discussing Musical Philosophy, Meta-psychics, Life, Birth. Death, and Sex, . and then playing with him. I literally thought my head was going to EXPLODE. I really felt like I was experiencing a physical extension of my Brain. (to be continued)

Back to DIZ, . (and down the road I'll tell the story about when OC and DIZ crossed paths) . . .

In this month's issue of Signal to Noise Magazine, . in the back is a full page cartoon featuring "Lil Matt Lavelle", . as he crosses paths with Jazz Icon Dizzy Gillespie. I sent the true story to a great illustrator, . Ben Towle, . who really hooked it up. We condensed it, . so I figure it's time for the total story to be revealed. (I cant believe this wasn't the first story I ever wrote.)

Me and 2 close friends went to see DIZZY at the Blue Note in NYC, . and it was the first time I had ever seen a Major Jazz figure in person, . or the first time I would even go to a Major Jazz club. (1988?) Blue Notes weird seating was in effect, . and the menu with Jazz names, . . . "A night in Tunisia", . for fried calamari was in effect to, and yeah expensive. Years Later I would play the jam session here several times, . which deserves ANOTHER blog.

So I'm in the front, . . . RIGHT under Dizzy's bell, . and there he is, . so close I could touch the Horn, . one of the co-creators of BOP, . and one of the greatest trumpet players who ever lived, . playing wrong better than the greatest right players could ever play right. Diz told the sold out house, . . . "Now a song I know better than anyone, . and played more than anybody. I should know, . . . I wrote it, . welcome to, . . . A Night in Tunisia" . . .

I quickly was lost completely in the music, . so much so that logical thought was out the window. The band was on FIRE for about 40 minutes. During the concert, Diz went to empty his spit valve, . but didn't know where to, . "make the drop", . being so close to the edge of the stage. I was right there with an empty coffee cup, . and without thinking, . pushed it under his bell, . like, . . . "Go ahead, . you can empty it in here . . ."

Dizzy Gillespie then stopped the show, . . . and saw an opportunity to have some fun, . by looking at me like, . . . "what, . . . is this guy nuts?" Maybe I am, . . . Maybe I was, . and the whole Blue Note decided that whatever I was, . this was some Funny shit . . .

HA HA HA HA HA HA HA HA HA HA HA!!!!!

Everybody was looking at me now, . but I was still in a music trance . . .

"NO YOU DIDN'T!" . . .

After the show, . my friend passed diz on the stairs to the dressing room and said, . "I'd Like to apologize for my friend . . ."

"Strange motherfucker that guy, . . . he might be sick . . ."

I went upstairs to the dressing room anyway to try and follow through. I'll never forget what I saw . . .

A bunch of Latin cats had a Conga player that wanted to join the band, . . . and were introducing him to Diz . . . "Does he have it?", . Diz asked, . . .

That's when the conga player got down on one knee in front of diz who was seated like a king on a throne. the cat opened his arms, . opening his heart and smiled . . . Diz said, . . . "We'll try him out" . . . Jon Faddis was in the room talking about having been in the studio all day, . I could tell that he and Diz were tight . . .

I said some random nonsense about Thank you for being a living legend, . and I play trumpet to . . .

When Diz heard that I played trumpet, . his WHOLE vibe changed, . and he stood up from the chair with a big smile, . . .

"Trumpet Players are coming out the woodwork, . I'll have to hear you some time . . ."

I don't remember much else, . but I do remember MAX ROACH asking me to help him find a Louis Armstrong version of "smile", . at Tower one day, . and I told him I was a trumpet player.

"You play?", . . . Max Roach then gave me his card and number and said, . . . "Call me when your playing and I'll come check you out, . . . I'm serious".

I kept that card for years, . but never felt I was ready to call Max Roach down to check me out, . . . after CLIFFORD, . and BOOKER, . . . shit. I had David Murray's card for years to, . to play through his transcription of Paul Gonsalves great 28 chorus blues solo, . but I never went . . .

I DO, . . . however, . . . still have a certain Coffee cup . . . a VERY, . . . special cup . . .

*dedicated to the Cecil Taylor backstage hang out I experienced while his big band played the IRIDIUM. When the band comes back, . . . am I in man? I promise I'll bring THE PLUNGER.

The Abandonded Sound

I was down in Battery Park in NYC several months ago around 2am watching the rhythm of the night river under a sliver crescent moon. All the way at the end of the walking path where you can see the statue of Liberty in the distance,. they have Blue Lights around a garden area that may have its inspiration in the architecture of Japan,. in a spiritual sense.

I thought I was alone until I heard a heavy sigh behind me and looked to see a woman wearing a cloak with a hood covering her. Her body Language suggested despair and defeat. I could not see her face but could feel the weight of her Melancholy emotion. I felt an uncontrollable desire to speak to her and offer my assistance.

Me: "Excuse me, . . . are you all right? is there anything I can do?"

Woman: "There is nothing anyone can do now . . ."

Me: "Why?,. what has happened?"

Woman: "They have left me. I have been abandoned" . . .

Me: "By who? Where are you from?"

Woman: "I am from the TONE WORLD".

. . . .

Me: "The tone world!?!, . . . What is your name if I may ask? I would like to Help!."

With that the woman lifted her weary head and looked over to me making eye contact, but she had no face! I could FEEL and HEAR her. I knew we were looking into each others SOUL.

Woman: (softly) "My name is Alto, . . . Alto Clarinet . . ."

. . . .

Me: (with a great deal of concern), . . . Alto?, . . . my name is Matt,. and I'm a musician.

Why would you say that? What has happened to you?

Alto: there have been only a few attempts to bring me Life,. and there is only one person in this vibration who helps me sing my song. I have a VITAL color,. and a VITAL message that I can bring.

No one has been able to hear me. The Tone world sent me here many years ago,. but with not enough people to give me life,. I am unable to truly exist,. and thus I am losing my life force at a slow, . . . painful rate.

"I am, . . . the abandoned Sound" . . .

. . . .

Me: "Not just yet"

Alto: (looking up at be cautiously,. with the feeling of Hope), . . .? "How so,. can You help me?"

Me: "Oh, . . . I can do a whole lot more than that . . . Come With Me!. I promise I will do everything in my power to help you complete your mission, . . . no, . . . OUR mission now.

Alto: "Who are you, . . . REALLY?"

Me: I play trumpet and Bass Clarinet. I know the only person who can really play you now. Being that it's 2am,. your being here makes perfect sense. 2am is the time of night that IS you. If it were 4am,. I would expect to find bass clarinet here. I have a direct contact with your people in the tone world and those responsible for the evolution of your integrity here, . . . and our meeting here can be no accident. I am a spiritual representative of the Blackwood. You can trust me,. I promise! Your being Lost should never have happened."

Alto: (with sadness),. But are the people ready for me now?"

Me: "Its now or never,. come on,. We Got This." . . .

With that, . . . Alto gently placed her hand in mine and gingerly stood up from the bench.

Alto: "where shall we go?"

Me: (smiling, . . . leaving no doubt that she can trust me), . . .

"Come!, . . . with your help I can complete my quest as well."

"Our future awaits" . . .

GONSALVES!

When someone asked Duke Ellington what he thought of the avant garde,. he replied . . .

"For the avant garde,. I have Paul Gonsalves . . ."

HAH!

Always looking for clues to the what's REALLY up in jazz,. I struck gold when I read this.I even wrote to DOWNBEAT pressing my case that Paul be elected to their Hall of Fame. They said no, but printed my letter,. which "fixed" the letter they printed that I wrote when I was 16 in 1986 claiming that Maynard Ferguson's NON high note playing was the greatest of them all.In search of moving further and further away from my heroes,. (I really agree with Matthew Shipp on how twisted we are in Jazz with our worship jones),. I'm gonna reveal full disclosure on my true favorite musician, . . . PAUL.(and keep on gravitating towards my own SUN.)When your coming up,. one way to go against the grain is to really get into the music of somebody on a different instrument,. although I never thought about it like that then.

I do believe I am the number 2 greatest living fan of Paul on Earth, . . . trumped only by a doctor in England who created a Paul Gonsalves website.(I'm NOT making a Paul myspace page,. that's a little kooky.)My man in England sent me cd-r copies of every record Paul did outside of Ellington,. and were talking almost TWENTY.I've paid people to transcribe solos of his,. not to learn or memorize,. but to put on my wall as ART.I've gone to record auctions and thrown down BIDS to get original copies of his 3 records on Impulse,. and also had a a guest DJ set on WBGO once to do a seminar on just why Paul is so BAD,. getting them to add more Paul to their play lists.(I did this on WKCR once to getting a phone call from a listener who said, . . . "Thanks man,. I never knew".) My relationship with WBGO went SOUTH when DJ and drummer Kenny Washington made me a deal: "If you write a letter to the program director telling him why BGO is WHACK,. then I'll play the Paul Gonsalves solos with Dizzy's big band,. (which I looked for for years).I wrote the letter,. pissing them off,. but was able to record those Paul/Dizzy tracks off the radio on to cassette. To top it all off,. I was even getting tight with MICHAEL JAMES, . . . Duke's nephew,. when we met at Tower Records.I made a copy of every record Paul ever did and called up Mike so I could give them to him,. and we planned a listening party,. where we would invite Tenor players,. (We were both friends with Harold Ashby),. when suddenly Mike passed on . . . (right around the time My friend HILTON RUIZ was murdered in New Orleans,. post Katrina,. really fucking me up.)

So what is it bout' Paul?,. (called "Mex",. in the band with Duke,. even though he was Portugeese.).((I'll never forget this argument I had with a great jazz singer named Eugene, when I living in the Jersey city YMCA, and he saw my poster of Paul on the wall,. about whether Paul was black)).Well, . . . for me,. Paul has always been the road map through Jazz so I never got stuck like those Lincoln center Ghouls.I CAME UP in swing by spending several years in a band with SIR HILDRED HUMPHRIES,. as my first real musical relationship,. and based on that,. I could have turned into one of those "revivalist" guys,. trying to play swing era music my whole life even though I WASN'T ALIVE THEN.Hildred always said that he thought Coltrane "was the greatest of us",. putting both of them in the same house,. and with a green light like that,. I didn't run from what I always heard from Paul Gonsalves, . . . FREEDOM.

In DUKE's band . . . His MAIN soloist . . . playing ideas that defy straight time and harmony,. REALLY well.Paul Gonsalves created a completely original sound language,. and then spoke it right at the heart of Duke Ellington's sound world for YEARS.Yes,. he dropped Ben Webster on Duke to get the job,. but he quickly moved on.Don't forget that before Duke,. Paul was BASIE's main tenor man for 4 years,. and spent a year with DIZ, . . . with TRANE on ALTO.According to Michael James,. Paul said he took Trane aside when they where with Dizzy and said, . . . "Man, . . . Tenor is your path,. go with the Tenor" . . . Paul was also playing

SHEETS OF SOUND then,. before Trane,. with Trane right there. Paul would also play the first true extended solo in jazz history,. the famous NEWPORT concert,. where he almost caused a RIOT,. and RE-IGNITED Duke's career. Then there's the fact that HILDRED was with BASIE for a few years,(Basie got him a gold plated tenor to get him to stay on the road). All this stuff is coming together. Oh yeah, ... that record I have with ARCHIE SHEPP SITTING IN WITH DUKE. (Cat Anderson's response on trumpet is beyond.catagory.)

FLASHBACK!!.

IT'S A PUBLIC DEBATE AT JALC IN THE EARLY 90'S.

WYNTON MARSALIS VS JAMES LINCOLN COLLIER.

The source of the debate, ... Collier's book on Duke has challenged Wynton's views,. and they have decided to settle up in a PUBLIC DEBATE. I'm in the Front row sitting with Stanley Crouch and Albert Murray,. (this is a true story). I'm an unknown trumpet player living in the Jersey city YMCA,. so broke I'm eating at homeless shelters and shit. I'm not there to join in on this public BASHING of Collier,. (man,. the WHOLE house was against him),. I'm there to DEFEND PAUL,. because in his book,. Collier dismissed him. During the public exchanges during the debate,. I kept raising my hand but being denied a chance to speak,. and I was getting tight. Albert Murray stopped the whole thing,. and told the moderator,. "let this young man speak!,."

So I challenged Collier on dismissing Paul,. and he responded, ... "I'm sorry,. but he's just not as creative as a COLEMAN HAWKINS or PRES ... "WHAT?", ... Wynton stepped in and said that Collier couldn't hear what Paul was doing and stressed that that was an opinion. I blanked out after that.(Did they carry me from the room?) ... The last thing I remember was Jimmy Knepper schooling the whole room on something. I guess if you roll with MINGUS like that,. people need to stop and listen ...

But that was then ...

I kept listening to Paul, . . . (whom David Murray cites as a key influence as well). Anybody reading and wants to go deeper,. track down any version of Ellington playing a tune called UP JUMP . . . "And now, . . . ladies and gentleman,. Paul Gonsalves practices Tenor saxophonic calisthenics in UP JUMP." . . . What follow's is a blazing fast,. totally augmented vehicle for Paul to basically play as fast and hard as he possibly can the entire piece,. ending in a solo cadenza,. where his DNA is laid bare before the whole world. Imagine,. as a musician,. playing in front of thousands of people,. standing down front of Duke Ellington's band,. and it's all bout' you. Not just you,. but your ultimate music,. your supreme chops, . . . SOLO. YOU GOT THIS. Duke was Paul's biggest fan then and even did an entire record to feature him,. which never happened to any other Ellingtonian. Duke also revealed his DARK side,. and why the DEVIL card in the tarot lines up with his birthday,. (along with the LOVERS),. by having Paul play UP JUMP when he was BOMBED . . . telling the audience afterwords with some delight,. "Paul Gonsalves!, . . . Drunk again!."

For many writers and musicians,. it was Paul's ability to get high,. (he was charter member of a group inside the band called the "Air Force"),. that they think of and remember. I choose to take the Gary Giddins perspective in his great book on BIRD, . . . that Paul's life and music are a TRIUMPH over the ADVERSITY of Drugs, booze,. and in Paul's case, . . . even ACID . . . (Which according to Jaee Logan,. is what took Giuseppe out)

Any other folks out there want to go deeper still,. check out Paul's Riverside album,. "Getting Together" . . . a NO Duke vibe . . . Let's see, . . . Well get Jimmy Cobb and Wynton Kelly from MILES,. and Nat Adderley and Sam Jones from CANNONBALL,. and then feature PAUL. (12/20/1960,. my fathers birthday) This is the only record I ever got SIGNED,. (by Jimmy and Nat),. and with good reason: It proves my case that Paul is one of the Tenor Masters. I'm not going to go all tech like Steve Coleman did with Bird,. I just need to Hear what went down,. not so much as see it.

IN closing,. my sermon ends today with a recollection of my prized possession. A video tape of Duke giving a lecture at the University of Wisconsin,. about a year before both he and Paul would leave this world,. within days of each other. After about 45 minutes of

Duke speaking and answering questions,. he seems slightly surprised that Paul has joined him on stage. "Ladies and Gentleman, . . . this is Paul Gonsalves" . . . Paul seems to be in another world,and waves off the microphone,. as they agree to play the ballad feature,. Happy Reunion" . . .

What follows is what many people playing free today are searching for:Those moments when the music comes together in a way that transcends the structure or the key,. and the music and we become ourselves.You need to play with a musical family to get there. No different than Paul's solo on "Praise God and dance",. from Duke's Live Second Sacred Concert,. which I believe proves that the avant garde and swing schools are really the same thing,. and that Jazz might be the biggest dysfunctional family of all time.

One day we'll get that Happy.Reunion.

The Great Trumpet Tree,. and Beyond . . .

April 1947 Freddie Webster falls to a supposed laced heroin dose meant for Sonny Stitt at age 31

July 1950 Fats Navarro falls to a combination of Tuberculosis and heroin at age 26

June 1956 Clifford Brown falls in a car accident at age 25

October 1961 Booker Little falls to Uremia at age 23

February 1972 Lee Morgan is shot and killed at age 33

May 1989 Woody Shaw falls in a brutal combination of tragic circumstances at age 44

Can anybody say the trumpet is not the most dangerous instrument in Jazz? There are many other people on this list that never even got a chance to document their music. The people I mentioned above besides Freddie Webster,. all were able to leave recorded legacies to some degree. Fats, Clifford the Comet, and Booker played more trumpet in their short lives than most of us will over an entire lifetime. I cant shake the fact that they had such small windows,. and were able to say so much,. establishing themselves as major parts of the horn's evolution. To play the trumpet this way calls for what I call a great deal of spiritual power,. and It's almost as if they KNEW they were only going to have a minute to say what they had to say,. and did everything they could to give their music life, . . . almost as if they gave their music part of their actual Living Life force. You can just hear so much LIFE in their sounds. A horn players Sound,. the TONE,. what comes out of the bell is the SOUND OF THEIR LIFE. These trumpet players and several others had so much to give us.The recordings we have of some of our fallen brothers shortly before their ascendancy are really dark,. so much Life just POURING out the bell,with time just running out on them.I've often thought that some musicians reach a vibration so high through their music that they just cant stay down here in the low vibration we continue to TOIL in.

Freddie Webster is hard to track,. but I did find him playing a solo on a song with Sarah Vaughan singing with a full orchestra,. confirming his influence on MILES.Dizzy also was quoted as saying he had one of the greatest trumpet sounds he ever heard.His influence on Miles can't be underestimated,. leaving space and putting your sound up front.Freddie sounds like Miles without the darkness,. although it was the Darkness that took him down.

FATS . . .While Fats is not one of my main inspirations,. I cant deny what a great player he was.Writers,critics,and historians are all totally off the mark saying he was "known for his great middle register playing",.suggesting he didn't go much deeper.I have recordings of Fats at Full power FLYING above high C above the staff,. almost rivaling DIZZY himself.I will even challenge MILES in his book saying Fats "Couldn't play a ballad for shit".I've tracked down a ballad by Fats on tour with the JATP,. and you can hear the audience holding their breath during a brief solo cadenza that reveals just a little bit of the impending tragedy heading his way.Fats TONE,. was actually FAT to me,. kind of like a lot of melted butter on hot toast,. or that chocolate syrup drowning your sundae.He went out playing,. and people are befuddled by a recording of him live with BIRD 2 weeks before his death.Maybe the date is wrong,. maybe not,. His range and power weren't 100%,. but either way,. he was broadcasting live on the air standing next to BIRD,. and he held his ground as well as Miles or KD.His lines might not have been CRACKLIN',. but they taste just fine to me.To rise up and play live with BIRD 2 weeks before you leave this world calls for yes, . . . Spiritual. power.Fats never got to hear the changes coming to Jazz years later,. and we can only wonder how he would have responded.I wish I could have heard him LIVE . . .

CLIFFORD the Comet . . .

I have a cassette of a live date with Max Roach(Max and Clifford had a special musical relationship)that I have never found elsewhere that has the best trumpet version of "Whats New?",. I have ever heard, . . . with Clifford playing long solo cadenzas,. and playing one of the FULLEST low F#'s ever played.(Miles,Wynton,Raphe,and myself have been known to reach downstairs in this way).On the bridge,. Clifford just reaches up to a G above high C, . . . at the perfect time,. rising with the musical moment.It has to be one of the best examples of how,why,and when to play up there ever recorded.

Booker's early passing at just 23 still stings to me,. even though it was 9 years before I was BORN.Booker was poised to do everything I have tried to deal with today before he left us.What he left is just straight INCREDIBLE.Of all of these guys,. Booker's is my Favorite Sound.It's so BURNISHED.Like AMBER.It's so TRUMPET.Booker worked on classical trumpet before he left to join Max Roach,. and had what I call one of the best Trumpet sounds,. getting into the horn itself.He had just enough of that BULL FIGHTING vibe,playing the horn for what it actually is,. that call to arms,. the signifier,. the testimonial. In short,. showing us that through it's sound,. that the Trumpet is CLOSER TO BIRTH AND DEATH THAN ANY OTHER HORN.In an interview he did that I found online,. he speaks of how he planned to investigate the natural quarter tones all over the horn.I became obsessed with those quarter tones and did a full study of them a few years ago,. but Booker was already there.I showed Ornette what I was doing and he said,. "You've found a new way to play music, . . . stop proving it and start applying it." Booker also speaks of the beauty of dissonance,. and he proved to be a great,original composer.Has anybody dealt with dissonance like him since then,. the way he was using it? Dave Douglas is a big fan of Booker,. and a serious composer as well,. we can connect Dave to Booker on the "tree".My favorite Booker moments are his SHAKE,. on AGGRESSION,. live at the Five spot with ERIC,. and his solos on Scoochie and Cycles from his sides with Booker Ervin. Timeless.Booker leads off his final record, . . . weeks before his death,. with a great piece called Victory and Sorrow.His victory in living his life,. yet the sorrow to leave,. and our sorrow that he left.

Who doesn't have their favorite LEE MORGAN moments? A Night in Tunsia live with Dizzy's big band, Tunisia again with Art Blakey in the studio, It's Only a Paper Moon live with Blakey, and CEORA in the studio,. are mine. LEE gives me that connection to the BLUES. The Attitude. THE BRASHNESS. Sometimes I just hear LEE cursing people out right from the horn. (I've heard Roy Campbell jr. do this to.) Clifford had some blues,. but Lee had some STREET. You can feel his music in your BLOOD,. in your pulse. Lee could just DANCE on the horn to me,. so much style. He had a different relationship with the trumpet than Booker and Clifford,. the role of the ADVERSARY: YOUR TOUGH,. BUT I CAN TAKE YOU DOWN ANYWAY. I don't want to say Macho,. but there is a vibe that if you don't like his music,. you just might get SLAPPED. Art Blakey was the PERFECT drummer for him. (Trumpet players LOVE great drummers,. we NEED and FEED each other.) Lee got to stick around a little longer and record a LOT more than the other guys,. but at 33,. he fell almost on some street shit, . . . getting shot by one of his ladies. Everybody knows the story,. (check out the latest book on Lee for the play by play). Lee told Roy Campbell that he was tired of hard bop and was getting into the open vibe more and more before he left us. He was continuing to EVOLVE his music when he was taken out.

WOODY. Somebody needs to write a book on Woody,. a favorite among SO many of us today. Woody made it to 44 before leaving,. I was 19 in 1989 when he left town. I always associate him with the 70's,. even going so far as to say he was THE trumpet man of that decade,. straight OWNING it. His interval playing forever changed everybody playing today,. and I wouldn't even exist if Woody didn't open that door. WIDE intervals were my entire operation before I started studying with OC. Woody left a sign for me that said,. "This way man!,. over here!."

ESCAPE VELOCITY is my favorite woody track,. his time feel was something,. just enough SMOOTH. Woody's music was kind of like where Fats, Clifford, Booker, and Lee might have been headed to,. He really just EVOLVED the entire conception of what was possible. Roy Campbell was tight with Woody as well,. giving me a slight connection to him through my friendship with TAZZ. Woody is Deep in that he's influenced many, many players,. but he's almost impossible to really imitate,. his thing was so personal. I can start running down fourths in all the keys,. but Woody had such a unique harmonic language and approach that you really cant get close enough to be a mark. A true innovation,. showing us a way out of the past into the future,. and demonstrating that it's possible to create a sound world almost entirely your own. Even when he was young,. I cant detect much influence of the trumpet players before him. Coming out yourself that quickly denotes a spiritual FOCUS that you have to bring with you when your born. Woody was actually allowed to stay with us 21 years longer than Booker Little,. but still left in the worse way,. which I wont get into detail about here,. whoever writes the book on him should find out the details of what really went down. Sometimes Life gets even ROUGHER than usual.

Playing trumpet seems to somehow push all of us a little closer to the edge. It's living your life a little louder than everybody else,. and reminding the world you exist every time you play. One thing the trumpet has always been able to do is make people pay ATTENTION. Hopefully this study hasn't been TO dark. I celebrate trumpet players that got to LIVE longer to. THAD JONES and NAT ADDERLEY are two of my favorite sounds. Needless to say,. those of us playing in 2010,. are quite ALIVE,. and spend quality time with the horn on the DAILY,. trying to spread good news,. I hope.

Here's to the masters we lost,. and those of us striving to be COMETS today. This is OUR time in the SUN,. believe it not . . .

Sex Jazz Life Blues

Louis Armstrong, . . . Pops, . . . wrote a blues that blew the spot on what Jazz really is,. and where it REALLY comes from.Just like the Bible,. the story of Jazz has become has been interpreted over and over again so that it makes sense to the people telling the story. (Uh-oh, . . . I'm about to do the same thing,. but I'm gonna get real on us).I'm going to go through the lyrics of the song that maybe destroyed my life,. but saved my soul,. by sending me on a life long pursuit of life coming through a trumpet.The song,. the Back O Town Blues . . .

"I had a woman, . . . Livin' way back o' town . . ."

BOOM.Right off Louis blows the spot on himself.Honesty with yourself is paramount to your music,. or you'll never get to your musical emotional core.It's no secret that Louis first woman was from the streets,. and may have been a prostitute, . . . It's also no secret that Louis MOM had to prostitute at times,. yes,. in order to survive.His father split early on and Louis supposedly only saw him in parades.(that would make a great scene in a film). That's where Jazz comes from if you subscribe that Louis taught the world to swing.

Louis married Daisy Parker in 1918.They adopted a 3-year-old boy, Clarence Armstrong, whose mother, Louis's cousin Flora, died soon after giving birth. Clarence Armstrong was mentally disabled (the result of a head injury at an early age) and Louis would spend the rest of his life taking care of him.The marriage to Parker failed quickly and they separated. She died shortly after the divorce.

DAMN.You know if you take Louis Armstrong's true birthday and break it down through numerology,. you get the Lovers card.How much Love can one man have inside him to take care of someone else when you can barley take care of themselves? What kind of man has the heart to RISE above it all? It was music that saved his life and showed him a way out, . . . a path that would make him no less than a cultural icon . . . Duke: "Louis Armstrong was born poor, died rich, . and never hurt anyone along the way".

Going even deeper, . the relationship between Jazz and SEX is really a HUGE part of the real story. Sex and Jazz have been lovers from the start. In truth Jazz was BORN because the slaves got down with the European classical thing to a degree, . just enough to set it off, . . . just enough so that when Louis Armstrong was a kid, . he wanted a Cornet, . to set him free. Your music is your life, . and this is the life that Louis came from, . where Jazz comes from.

In short, . Jazz would not exist unless many, many people suffered a great deal. All that pain and suffering had to go somewhere, . and buried somewhere really deep in the story of the human being is our ability to do just that. The ability to CREATE our way out of pain. Louis Armstrong did more than teach the world to swing, . he taught us what we actually can be when faced with ourselves.

"Yeah she treated me right, . Never let me down . . .

But I wasn't satisfied, .

I had to run around" . . .

Ok, . now the tune takes a solemn turn. What happened to Louis here is something I can relate to on a more personal level. Self destruction, . and taking chances, . RISK, . and CONSEQUENCE. I've risked it all to defeat an oppressive, crushing loneliness, . the kind that makes your breathing erratic. Both times I've paid a heavy price, . worse than any emotion I wasn't intelligent enough to control. But isn't RISK the very essence of Jazz? Its no coincidence when you take action in your life and in your music the exact same way. People's lives and music are usually quite similar . . .

"Now I'm worried as can be . . . Oh I've searched this world all over,. Wonderin' where she could be . . ."

Ok,. well,. once you mess up like that in a relationship,. people sometimes VANISH on you,. but these days people vanish all the time for far more reasons that,. ducking out of relationships either cause their afraid,bored,tired or all three.In truth,. I would imagine that Daisy was someone to worry about,. and in fact she died not long after her and Louis were done.(whew!),. . . DEATH was just in everybody's business so much back then,. seems everybody had a shorter life span and just had a rougher,more extreme life, . . . again,. the world that Jazz was born into.

"I would ask that she forgive me . . . And maybe she'll come back to me . . . **spoken**(but I doubt it) . . . I'm lonesome an blue,. And I've learned a thing or two, . . . Oh fellas here's a tip I'm gonna pass on down to you, . . . Never mistreat your woman . . . Cause it's gonna bounce right back on you . . ."

The heart of life is learning a lesson about yourself and life from experiences like this. The blues is filled with these moments,. and its that connection to life that is missing in so much Jazz today.So much Jazz today has no RISK,. and no LESSON learned,. no LIFE behind it.Many veterans tell me,. "If you cant play the blues,. you cant play Jazz",. and I pride myself on being able to do just that.Play the BLUES.It was Louis Armstrong's trumpet solo on Back O Town Blues that told me to get a horn and start wailing.To this day,. I'll never forget the feeling I got when he just started pouring blues all over the place,. right out the horn.

Unfortunately for me,. the greatest music I have ever played was always in reaction to something going down between me and a woman.Something about what happens when we try and get together that still resonates at the very highest and lowest levels of our art,. and mine imparticular.My music and the music of many others,. in all kinds of music resonates with this struggle.

You see,. the trouble is that Madam ZZAJ herself actually is a woman, . . . that seduced me entirely many years ago . . .

"You know Matt, . . . when we go to bed at night,. you might as well curl up next to that damn TRUMPET,. since you Love her more than me!!"

Or worse, . . . holding my trumpet outside a 5th story window,.

"How about I just DROP this shit? would you jump right after it!?"

In truth I did jump into the subway tracks to save my bass clarinet once.

But I'm still HERE.

Thanks Pops . . .

I'll be seeing you soon enough . . .

*Dedicated to Trummy Young, Barney Bigard, Nina Simone, and Larry Roland,. (who knows the right way to define Divine inspiration!!)

KING ERIC

When people hear music that touches their soul,. you can usually see a reaction of some kind. Whenever I'm in a musical situation,. I look to see who's feeling what's going down.Some folks sit quietly and maybe their eyes water.Some close their eyes and try to internalize the experience. Some just smile and nod their head in approval(hopefully).In some music people jump into Mosh Pits and in other music people hold up lighters en mass.(Jazz people are to serious and controlled for that shit).

It's the physical reaction I seek,. because that means what's inside you is resonating strong enough that your body has to react.It's not a choice like,. "I think I'll let my head shake in reaction to this music",. it just HAPPENS.The music playing IS what you are on some level,. there's something inside of it that is telling you "this way! over here!",. in a manner where the validity or the truth behind is is not questioned,. it just IS.

In short, . . . what's that music that makes you DANCE? . . . Makes your soul just DANCE . . .

In my favorite movie,. Awakenings,. they play music to help wake people up that have a condition where they simply sleep for most of their lives,. never able to wake up.(Dexter Gordon plays one of the patients!).In my favorite scene,. they keep trying different music to help them wake up,. and this one white guy doesn't react all all until they play HENDRIX,. It's the only music that reaches in beyond his illness.

I bring this up because the only music that really makes me DANCE is Eric Dolphy and John Coltrane.I Love lots of music,. but these 2 guys actually make me get up out the chair and just DANCE.I simply cant hide my reaction to their music every time I hear it,. and I have soul-danced to Trane live at the Vanguard well over 1,000 times,. my desert island record.People on the subway see me doing this all the time,. I just cant help it. Just What is this about? As much as I have written about Trane,. Eric D was right there,. they were BROTHERS.

I have always struggled to explain my relationship to Eric Dolphy's music in words. After listening to him since 1987,. and playing Bass Clarinet without a doubt,. because he set it off,. for about 11 years now,. I have reached the conclusion that I simply have never been the same since the first time I ever heard him.

In 1987 I was 17 and a was fast becoming a fan of jazz,. and had just begun getting a little serious,. renting a videotape to see Trane,. who I knew very little about.(I have several friends today who got to see him live,. but alas, . . . not me).I had no idea who Eric Dolphy was, . . .

Then it just happened . . .

After Trane got down on Impressions,the camera suddenly shifted to this guy on alto who was PLAYING THE IMPOSSIBLE . . .

. . .

What the Hell?!? He was ALL over the horn,. reaching ABOVE and BELOW,. he was talking a language from the future nobody had ever heard . . . SWEEPING, SWOOPING,and SCOOPING below,. REACHING, PREACHING, AND TEACHING ABOVE.

Eric Dolphy was Dancing,. and I simply would never be the same.

2005

Ornette Coleman's house, . . . Jam session in progress, . . . I'm trying like hell to impress OC with my ULTIMATE shit.

STOP.

My heart falls out of my chest and just hits the ground bleeding on the floor. I'm as open and vulnerable as I have ever been in my life trying to get OC to hear my song,. and something has gone wrong, . . . horribly wrong as I'M the reason he just STOPPED THE MUSIC.

"You didn't resolve your idea . . . why? . . . Why would you say something you don't mean? Would you stop talking in the middle of a sentence?"

"I know what your sound is,. and now your playing like somebody I don't know,. why?"

2006

Back at Ornette's,. and I run out of ideas,. and do a LONG glissando on the upper register of the bass clarinet,. almost a fifth,. Hodges style . . . reaching for my vocal thing that Eric set off . . .

STOP

"How can you resolve an idea without notes?"

"But Eric, . . ."

"That's Eric man,. not you"

At this point OC left the room and brought me back my trumpet from the other room.

"Use this,. and you won't hear that stuff anymore"

2010

It took me several years to answer these question's that OC presented,. and it all comes back to that initial moment when Eric Dolphy basically showed me that "This is what music is to ME" . . . (Those damn wide intervals don't resolve so easily!)

Having your own language in music is a monumental achievement,. and Eric may have the most personal dialect of them all,. one that wouldn't exist if BIRD didn't exist.I have pursued my own language with an actual focus and purpose thanks to OC,. and the bottom line is that Eric's soul dance has always been right at the very heart of what I would call my ultimate relationship to music.The way he plays the lower register is the reason I had to get a Bass Clarinet,. and why I have always been conflicted in finding the right horn and the right notes FOR ME.I'm still trying to speak with a human voice on the horn sometimes too,. just not around Ornette.

ED did this to me in a matter of seconds from a concert he did in Germany with Trane,. something he may have quickly forgotten about as he was clearly all about continuing his life of music.His music with MINGUS is SO important to me,. something that should be written about at length. Eric was ready to play with ALBERT before he left tragically.To me Eric is the consummate avant garde player in that his TECHNIQUE surpassed almost anybody in jazz from any period.To play the way he heard music takes a TREMENDOUS amount of chops.Going deeper still there's Elvin in the interview on that video tape saying,. "Then John brought in Eric and EVERYTHING changed". (Sonny Fortune told me that playing with Elvin was as close as music will ever get to Sex,. one of Ornette's favorite subjects)

Conclusion:King Eric and Trane are 2 of the main reasons I've dedicated my life to music.(maybe I'll get into the Louis Armstrong portion next)

As I listen to the complete Coltrane at the Vanguard while I write this,. I cant help but mention my life long dream,. playing the same place at a very different time.

Eric Dolphy and John Coltrane stood on that stage at the Vanguard and played music that is the foundation of my musical life.

One day, . . .

I will stand on that stage myself,. and sing MY song to the world.

Matt Lavelle

That's my WORD.

**dedicated to the great Marc Crawford,. writer, teacher,. Soul brother of the highest order

The Boston Jazz Party

Hey Lowell! Hey Cambridge!,. Yours truly is making his way up to Massachusetts this weekend to play at the 119 Gallery (Friday 12/11 at 8pm),. and at Outpost 186 (Saturday 12/12 at 8pm) I would Love to meet anybody that's read my blogs or into my music in a rare excursion outside of NYC with my own Music. I would like to collectively thank Chris Rich, John Voigt, Syd Smart, Walter Wright, and Rob Chalfen for being a part of OC's favorite thing,. the idea . . .

I was going to write about Linking the work of Neil Degrasse Tyson to Joe Henderson Live in Japan,. or maybe talk about all the non jazz projects I've done,. but going up to Massachusetts got me remembering my only time up in those parts, . . . so I'd Like to invite you to, . . . the Boston Jazz Party . . .

Quiet as it's kept,. but I'm outing myself here,. I was a student at the Berklee college of Music for one semester in the early 90's,. and in reflection,. I cant believe all the memories that came flooding back. The first thing I encountered was a cat on the phone in the hallway who would introduce me to the playing of a GEORGE GARZONE. To this day I've never said more than a few words with GG,. but what he was doing with music,. seeing him Live,. had MAJOR impact on me . . . His control of the lower register was the first sign that pointed downstairs to the Land of Bass-Clarinet . . .

The next thing I ran into was my friend to this day,. a fantastic trumpet Player named Gilbert Castellanos. Google him. Even then,. Gil had already crossed paths with Dizzy who could tell he was Mexican American by his sound. Gil was Already fluent in Bop,. and the first Trumpet player I ever met who was the real deal. We had another friend named Yanos who was like 17 and playing like Trane on the 50's Miles sessions,. sound and everything.

157

Both of these guys were on full ride scholarships,. but I was on a "partial",. as they gave me 1/3 of the tuition for my reading of Round Midnight I sent them on a cassette from a duo I had with an Old Piano player in New Paltz NY,. where I was prior studying art. I had another great roommate named Juan was was a great bass player and singer from Puerto Rico,. who told me about LA PERLA,. and spent a lot of time with me and his crew messing with a OUIJA BOARD

Berklee had to then rate me so I could be placed in ensemble's and I chose to play,. "I let a Song go out of my Heart",. and I Sucked. They sent me to the all beginner ensemble and I had to argue my way into a Latin Jazz class that you needed 3's to be in. One day Gil asked me to sub in the Art Blakey ensemble and I was scared . . .

Rightfully so,. as the teacher first dismissed me as not really being from NY because I couldn't play,. after not being able to sight transpose,read,and solo over Milestones,. (the original bop line where Bird played tenor). More than that I'll never forget how much the teacher hated Wynton's music,. saying,. with anger,. that he "Sounded Like Shit . . ." . . . I was still on the fence with no musical identity as of yet,. so that was heavy . . .

In a 4 month time span,. All of the following would go down,. before I ran out of Loan Money and was dismissed to learn Jazz on my own . . . (during the 4 months I sent my mentor Sir Hildred Humphries a post card saying,. "Your the real thing,. nobody here is playing anything" . . .) . . .

In Long Order,. Here's what my brain allowed me to recall:

I would knock a guy down in the street in a rush between my job in the School Kitchen and a Ear training class(I was better at serving food than sight-singing and conducting) . . . When I knocked him down,. a whole crew of guys came by on some power shit and made me leave . . . I had just knocked over one of the guys from NEW KIDS ON THE BLOCK,. and they all looked at me like they would Kick my ass . . . My boss in the Kitchen was a singer who told me Sarah Vaughan would be the best to sing Monk. Some guy that worked with me was always messing with me saying,. "Stop talking Like Louis Armstrong",. (My sister used to remind me that I wasn't POPS as well) . . .

I would run out of money and another Trumpet Player suggested we DONATE SPERM . . . We took a bus across town and filled out the papers. At 20 something I was actually considering it. When they found Out that all my grandparents died recently or early by Hardcore Terminal Medical things, they rejected me, . . . which didn't matter anyway,. when My Mother found Out I was down there she BECAME A DRAGON AND PUT THAT SHIT TO SLEEP . . .

And another Level Down . . .

They had a TOWER RECORDS where I got a Jobim compilation to learn "Desafinado",. which led me to fall in Love with ELIS REGINA . . . I failed a DIANETICS stress test,. and watched a Chick Corea video. They told me I was SUICIDAL,. and that Dianetics was the only way out . . . (I declined) . . . I played at a famous repair shop and Emilio told me I had a Sound . . . (Does he tell everybody that?) . . . One night there was what could be called some kind of GANG FIGHT between the guys from my building and some Local guys right on the street nearby. I don't remember why,. but in the melee I saw some guy get his Glasses destroyed,. which convinced me to stop fighting and bounce . . . I had 3 potential girlfriends and ruined everything with all 3 by,. 1) canceling a date to watch Giants/redskins on Monday Night football,. 2) trying to teach a trumpet player how to improvise when she wanted to actually * * * . . . 3) Not being able to get around a culture and Language barrier with a girl from the Middle east . . . (None of them are on Facebook thank god) . . . I would play at WALLYS,. (see my blog,. Thou Shalt Not Play Jazz) . . . One Night I was walking through the city Late, and alone. I walked by a phone booth,. and the Phone Rang,. so I picked it up. Some guy in a nearby building could see me from his window and asked me to come see him upstairs. (I RAN all the way home!) . . . I would get to know a Baritone sax player/composer now running a 40 something member hip hop jazz orchestra in Los Angeles . . . I would play my only concert in the mess hall during Dinner . . . After "Work Song",. and 1 original, . . . I was ambushed by 3 Horn players who wanted to turn it into a jam battle,. and they all took Long solos to prove I wasn't shit.One of the guys was an Alto player labeled as crazy for playing free! . . . I would meet a English cat who had almost Maynards chops and Paul Gonsalves ability to drink

And even further below . . .

I would encounter a street Musician in a Snow man costume,. that I could never understand because of the Mask,. but he or she was singing with a Mandolin or something . . . I got some great Paul Gonslaves records at a well known local shop, . . . and Lastly, . . . I would be broke,.AGAIN,. and need about $40 to get to the end of the week . . . when I looked down and found $40 AT MY FEET ON THE STREET . . .

And finally,.

I heard that Magic Johnson got AIDS which shook me up a little,. not sure why,. and then I got the news . . .

MILES DAVIS WAS DEAD . . .

Wait, . . . What?

. . . .

I found out on the street and went home to an empty room and felt Heavy,. Like Lead.I put on Miles playing a ballad with a Velvet-tone mute with Horace Silver on Piano,. I can never remember the title, . . .

But I remember what I did next, . . .

Which was to hang my head,. and Cry . . .

Thou Shalt Not Play Jazz

Everybody has Jam session stories,. me being no exception.Some times good things go down,sometimes bad,. sometimes necessary,. and sometimes, . . . unnecessary . . . I've Haunted a few,. and one particular one really stands out as above and beyond what can go down in these random attempts of people who may not know each other at all try to make music together in front of other musicians,tourists,and maybe some really tired,but hardcore listeners of Jazz . . .

Yes, . . . SMALLS,. in NYC was the spot in the early 90's for early 20-something musicians from anywhere on Earth to come and test themselves playing Jazz in the Jazz capitol of the world.

I have not been there since the mid 90's,. so I can't say what it's like now. When I was going,. It was to the all night jam session,. held every night.Maybe it's still going down.

I was living at that YMCA in Jersey city and used to crash Smalls as often as I could,. or as Long as I could stay awake.I had a 40 hour day gig at Tower records that started at 9am.I used to go to play at Smalls and sometimes sleep there from like 6:30-8am,. and then go to work.(hey,. when your like 23 you can pull off shit like this) . . .

The protocol was pretty whack.Wait until whatever band is playing finishes up around 2am,. and then get on the List,. or just try and get to know who's running the session and wait for the call.This means it might be 4am when you get 2 choruses on All the Things You are,. or that you might be able to get down and pick the tune,. or maybe,. you wont even play it all.Yes,. who you knew that was present was a major factor,. and the guys running the session had their crew up-front.If a celebrity cat showed up,. everything was out the window and they took over the session so everybody could experience how great they where.Do I sound bitter? Well,. here's where I'm going . . .

There's a Drummer that is fairly well known that is revered as part of what made Smalls great to those who really made this scene part of their lives long term,. his name? Jimmy Lovelace.Google him to find some Loving tributes about he's recent departure to the great Jam session in the sky.

Mr.Lovelace was an original,. and had some cred,. recording with Wes and was with Benson for over a decade.

However this is also the man that tried to get me to Quit Music outright.

During this time,. I was a so-so straight ahead trumpet player with a small list of tunes I had ready to go for Jam sessions.I'm not sure I had much of my sound.As I recall I had a big question at the time for myself, . . . which was,. what if I stepped outside the changes? Everybody there was on some tight-rope play by the rules type shit.Play IN and don't start no shit.My changes playing then was I said,. so-so.I had to play free for years to get good at playing changes I would learn later.I heard they asked Daniel Carter to leave Smalls once,. which he confirmed . . . "That's not what we do here",. he was told.(I didn't meet DC until years later.)

So one night I decided to find out what would go down,. more for my own quest of what music was than anything else,. and I went as OUT as I could.Just Played WILD and shit,. Think it was "There will never be another you",. which I actually was quite good at swinging on . . . But Not Tonight, . . . I just went for outer space,. My free Jazz peeps now would be proud of what I tried to do . . .

Jimmy Lovelace, . . . was not impressed . . .

"Come here man,. I want to talk to you", . . .

I had no idea who Jimmy was at the time,. except for the White suit he had on all the time. He was an older cat,. which to me meant Respect. He asked me to sit down so he could explain some things,. which I did . . . Jimmy then told me he was going to do me the biggest favor of my Life,. and tell me what I needed to hear.

"Music is not for you . . . You don't have it . . . the best thing you can do for your life right now is quit the trumpet and quit Music. I'm doing this for your own good" . . .

I listened and didn't know what to think. I didn't see that coming. I told Jimmy I appreciate that he would step to me like this,. that he was looking to help me. I tried to explain to him that I was trying to play outside of what the "rules" where,. that I liked to play IN sometimes to. He said he heard me play like that and still felt the way he did, . . . and that HE HAD THE RIGHT to tell me to walk away from Music forever . . . Hard not to think of AMERICAN IDOL,. JAZZ style . . . I went home.

That night I thought about what He asked me to do . . . QUIT MUSIC . . . Was he trying to get me to just get serious? Teachers sometimes brutalize students like boot camp to challenge or force them to get to their core. This violent method of teaching sometimes kills people's music. I've seen that happen in students from Berklee and the New School.

Arnie Lawrence,. the first Live Jazz Musician I ever saw play in person,. came into Smalls once and was cool,. telling me to study with Art Blakey trumpet man Valery Ponomerev,. but then Valery would decide to get Brutal as well,. saying that I should also "go to the new school or quit",. because my trumpet warm-up wasn't up to speed. (I've had an obsessive compulsive thing with warming up ever since) . . . I never asked Jimmy Lovelace for a lesson,. this was his "Gift" to me . . .

The next night,. what could only be my spiritual power,. still dormant,. sent me a message: "To take somebody away from their own music can cause Profound damage if that person's music is attached to their core development in a spiritual sense. Art or music can be part of a transformational process which has a direct hand in the evolution of someones soul.

Don't walk away from your Music unless your SOUL asks you to change direction,. and decisions like that are usually made between Lives"

So the next night after that,. I went back to Smalls and Jimmy was there. I played a few choruses on "There is no greater Love",. and then Jimmy started walking over with that,. "I thought I told you you couldn't play vibe" . . .

I told him with my horn in my hand, . . . "Step the Fuck away from me man,. or were going to Fight."

I was dead serious,. and felt that I was protecting my music,. protecting my soul. Jimmy backed off,. but as he did he said again, . . . "I was trying to help you" . . . He was frustrated . . .

Needless to say, . . . my time at Smalls was coming to an end . . . Another trumpet player wanted to fight me outside,. and I don't remember why,. all I remember is he had a big trumpet medallion hanging around his neck,. and he was actually a free cat. Before it was time to go however,. it was time for my Bright Moments, . . . kind of . . . here they are in quick succession, . . . a top 10 list like no other . . .

1) Frank Hewitt,. a great Piano player,. stopping the session and telling everyone, . . . "Clifford Brown needed 3 choruses tops to say what he had to say, . . . If you need more than 3,. You don't have anything to say".

2) Tommy Turrentine,. a great trumpet player cursing out the whole place,. "Nobody here is playing shit!!",., (Tommy may have Lived there for a minute)

3) Nicholas Payton playing GIANT STEPS at 4am with no piano,. then playing Bass,. and then drums! I was half asleep and didn't know Giant Steps anyway . . .

5) The great bassist Victor Gaskin playing longer than anybody and refusing to give up . . . He was yelling at me on "moments Notice",. COME ON MAN!,. (I got Lost on the bridge),. around 5am

We had no Piano on that one.

6) Playing a blues with Andy Bey on Piano . . . Andy was really listening and working with me. I left some space and then dropped the flat six and held it out, . . . Andy waited and then played the PERFECT CHORD AT THE PERFECT TIME, . . . I'll never forget it . . .

7) On a long train of Horn players on Bb rhythm,. having the 3rd bass player already,. I just FORCED a whole tone improv on everybody and got away with it! the rhythm section hooked up with me and afterwords Roy Hargrove was like, . . . Yeah man!" . . . Roy had forgotten that he DESTROYED me on Confirmation across town at Yarbird Suite,. and also on Mr. P.C. at the Blue note. Roy was cool.

8) arguing about what tune to play when some kid wanted to play Wayne Shorter's "Miako",. ending up on "What is this thing called Love", . . . and then the Piano player playing like Cecil Taylor to fuck with all the horn players on purpose

9) Calling Four in a key I didn't know it in,. and then being forced to play chromatic like crazy,. and then some tourists thinking I was playing my ass off . . . (maybe this happened at Mo' betters on the upper west side,. not sure)

10) Cherokee battles,. of course. Tempo and Key unknown till the downbeat . . . B sucks.

The Last time I Played at Smalls was with a Guitar player on Have You Met Miss Jones,. and I remember I got a lot of people to Listen,. and the owner,. a cool cat named Mitch,. said,.

"yeah Matt",. as I worked my way through the bridge.It was around 5am and the session ended after I stopped playing.I knew It was time to go.

After that I ran my own Jam session in Chelsea at a place called the Rainy Daze for about a year and half,. and started writing my own tunes and exploring 60's Miles.I met Francois Grillot,. who I still play with to this day on the free Jazz tip.My music found a way through that maze,. but It wasn't until I studied with Ornette and played with Sabir Mateen that it CRYSTALLIZED.Years,. and a Bass Clarinet Later . . . Oh yeah, . . . with a few Free Jazz Jam sessions to along the way,. (very dangerous)

The best Jam session I ever went to was run by Roy Campbell at the Lenox Lounge in Harlem.

After a scorching set of Woody Shaw tunes with his great band TAZZ,. the session started and

EVERYBODY WAS COOL . . .

Can somebody in please Boston Write about WALLY's?

Anyway, . . . thanks Mr.Lovelace, . . . for trying to show me the light,. and that . . .

Thou, . . . Shalt, . . . (Ahem!)

PLAY.

John Coltrane and the Great Choice to Be

I believe I have heard what may be one of the most important and defining moments in jazz history.For years now,. This live cut of Miles Davis with John Coltrane has haunted me. Many people have asked the question,. "Just what went down at the OLYMPIA anyway? In 1960,. Miles Davis had an incredible 21 or 22 day tour with his quintet in Europe,. playing EVERY night.(can anybody imagine getting a tour like this today? I know it was hard work for them,. but shit,. SIGN me the hell up!).We all know that this was Trane's last stand with Miles,. and that Miles had to work to get him to do it as Trane was already on the path to himself,. and that Trane told him this was his last call.What may we ask,. were the musical dividends?

All roads lead to Bye Bye Blackbird,. the second song after a run down of walkin',. (I always liked the Wayne versions better on that one.) Lets take apart and deconstruct the Blackbird with 2 things in mind . . . 1) that according to Lewis Porter,. Blackbird was dropped from the program the whole rest of the tour,. (the OLYMPIA was the first night),. and 2),. what Horace Silver told Dave Douglas,. in that many people get the wrong message from Trane:behind his relentless search and stacking up of chords on chords,. there was a beautiful voice leading going down.While that may be true,. I feel Trane was really on a quest to just SLASH and BURN anything in the way of him becoming, . . . TRANE.I think Trane became himself on this night in 1960,. on stage,. with Miles Davis,. in Miles band,. in front of a huge crowd in Europe.There were clearly pro and anti Trane forces in the house,. voiced by the crowd.(reminds me of Jameel Moondoc telling me about the Mary Lou Williams/Cecil Taylor concert . . . MOON,. who was there,. said the right side of the house was all Mary Lou.The left side,. C.T.) . . . Lets put blackbird under a musical microscope with my special lens,. and see if we cant strike GOLD.

After a very short,nice,polite Wynton Kelly piano intro,. ("Hi!,. come on in,. were not here to hurt anybody"),. Miles introduces us to the Blackbird,. a sweet,. and gentle Bird,. by playing the simple,gentle melody as only he can,. on harmon mute,. up close,. nice and tight,. on the microphone.In seconds we are all put on 100% notice,. we're in MILES WORLD,. it's his house,. and he starts the MUSICAL SEDUCTION.25 seconds in,. the crowd breaks into applause under the music.("This is why we are here,. we love being guests in Miles home,. were happy to be here").At the end of the first melody/chorus,. a nice easy break,. and we stroll through the park with Miles on a sunny day,. and the tempo is just perfect ... You can feel the sun on your skin,. and that gentle breeze,. oh,. just right.Miles stays with us for a full 5 choruses,. a great host.(Mr PC,Jimmy Cobb,and the Real Wynton are happy to oblige and serve us while were In Miles house).After the bridge on the last chorus,. Miles takes seven steps outside of character,. and plays a little more aggressively,. It seems there's a STORM coming on the horizon ...

At 4:50 we meet John Coltrane on the street,. and Brother John has a serious expression on his face ... (Is anything the matter man?,. are we cool?) ... The wind starts to pick up and the rustle of dead leaves that haven't been bagged yet can be heard.The Clouds are starting to block the sun,and the temperature drops just a hint.You could also call this a COSMIC SHIFT.(This is like the TECTONIC PLATES shifting to me).Trane introduces himself as a friend of Miles,. and shows us what they have in common.("I'm in Miles world,. just like you").Thus ends the first chorus with brother John.(Miles has gone to the kitchen to get us a beer perhaps,.)

On our second chorus,. John introduces us to 2 notes that don't resolve too well,. and everything starts to feel FAST,. even though the tempo is right where it was,. (and stays). ("Well,. now that we have been introduced,. let me show you what else I've found in here ... Miles doesn't look for this stuff,. but I HAVE to keep looking,. I LOVE finding things ...") John ends chorus 2 with 2 simple in tune blues phrases ... ("were friends right? Come with me a little further ...") It's like saying hello and goodbye at the same time.

Chorus 3,. John starts sending the little blackbird through some serious nosedives and rapid accents. Shes flying all over the place and really getting a workout,. almost like a warning of some kind. This is My Favorite Things level improv now . . . ("Now that we know each other a little bit,. it's time for you to meet my real self,. somebody I'm still getting to know a little better,. one note at a time")

Chorus 4: SHEETS of Sound are coming down,. and the sky opens up at last revealing a heavy rain. The birds sing even louder,. celebrating bath time. ("take shelter if you need to,. but this is where I'll be in Miles world at the moment,. I love it out here,. where I MUST be"). Wynton and the crew enter on the bridge and let us know they're still together and that everything is going to be OK. They back off again after the bridge,. and John almost resolves some of these torrential phrases.

Chorus 5: John is at the foot of the mountain top now, . . . ("I can see the top!! Lets go!!") He tries to continue the search in the upper register AND be miles lyrical at the same time! GOLD. The crowd tension rises,. which you actually hear. The unrest is palpable. ("Are you going to now take more choruses than Miles himself in his band!?,. This ISN'T why I came over today!,. wait,. do we like this? CAN we like this? Are we ALLOWED to like this? Miles!,. Is this OK?!!") (("I HOPE,. you brought your umbrella,. cause it's ON now.")).

Finally, . . . the CHORUS OF TRUTH,. and one of the BRIGHTEST moments in Jazz History,. chorus SIX,. (the Lovers card). The crowd now lets John know he's crossing the line. Everybody gathers around and stares at the line and John crossing the border,. LEAVING Miles world, . . . never to return(?). We reach the bridge at 9:37 and John reaches a strong note outside the safety zone,. a dangerous note. He chooses to NOT resolve it,. and then REPEATS it,. over,. and over. ("I HAVE GOT TO BEE FREEE,. I HAVE GOT TO BE FREE,. EVERYBODY LET ME BE,. SET MEEE FREEE.!") . . . and then at 9:50 after the bridge,. John goes to ANOTHER out note,. HIGHER, . . . LOUDER,. JAZZ AT THE PHILHARMONIC,. OUT STYLE,. He repeats and repeats. As the chorus ends,. the crowd ERUPTS . . . ("Well,. we have got to admire anybody willing to stand by their convictions in this way . . . In Miles house? You are a BOLD and STRONG man,. who has EARNED our Respect.) . . . and also . . . ("This is outrageous! How

dare Trane make me feel something differently? I'm angry and upset, because I'm AFRAID.")
((I have news for them, . . . John was gonna do what he had to do anyway . . .))

Chorus 7: Just outside of Miles World,. the crowd is in a state of chaos and a little panic . . .
TRANE is now HIMSELF,. and doesn't let up!! During the bridge,. the crowd again voices
their opinion,. and Trane turns down the heat. After the bridge,. Trane plays beautiful, lyrical
phrases,. in time,. in key, . . . and ends perfectly,. no different than Miles himself would . . .
("Thanks for taking this trip with me everybody,. I Love Miles too,. and could play like that if
I wanted to,. but I CHOOSE to be me") . . . There is no way,. I feel,. that John Coltrane knew
he was carrying the entire history of jazz on his shoulders,. and that his choice would have
impact on Jazz like an asteroid hitting Earth,. like BIRD,. and OC after that. (Everybody playing
today was there in a way,. I thought it was great,. but the lincoln center guys left pissed.)

After TRANE,. Wynton Kelly came by,. but the party was over. After 3 choruses,. he decided
to turn the lights off,. Miles comes in on the bridge, with a short, abstract version of the
melody,. and ends the Tune alone. Even Miles didn't know how to respond to what went
down,. and he starts off Round Midnight solo to regain control,. but, . . . the deed,. has been
done. FOURTEEN MINUTES had passed . . . and they had at least 20 more nights,. in a row,.
to continue this public conversation,. one of the most important in jazz history . . .

John Coltrane was now on a spiritual quest,. and music was his vehicle for transformation.
He would not stop,. as his music brought him closer to himself,. and closer to God,. one
note at a time . . . He had made the TRANSITION. Many of us traveled with him,. and some
of us still do . . . and now I can connect Trane to Louis Armstrong,. and let jazz become
itself: Louis made a record with Dave Brubeck called,. "the Real ambassadors",. and on
this record is a song called They say I look like God. In one of Louis Armstrong's brightest.
moments.,. he sings,.

Then God gave man,. the Great choice to be . . .

Alone on Earth, . . . or one, . . . with thee . . .

TOWER RECORDS

Taking a closer look at all the jobs I've had while pursuing Jazz,. Tower Records stands way above all of them. Tower was the greatest job I ever had. I was there for almost 10 years. Running the shipping and receiving department for 7 years, and then getting the gig as the JAZZ BUYER.

The what?

That's right,. I was the Jazz product specialist. I managed the top floor which we eventually moved to the basement. I was in charge of jazz in one of the greatest and well known record stores in the world,. in the so called jazz capital of the world,. NYC. Even deeper,. Jazz at Lincoln center was literally right next door,. but had no say in what we did. I could decide how and what we pushed to some degree. My manager then was a free thinking cat who wanted to really push the envelope and put us on the map in the city as an important part of the scene. This was a public place,. THE place where all people interested in Jazz came through. Having a direct connection to who I actually was during the day meant a great deal to me,. and I decided to take it all the way.

So what did I actually do? When I got the position Tower was all ready a victim of what was known as central buying,. which means a computer would order everything "important" for the store. Somewhere in Tower, not in the city,. all the decisions about product were made in regards to the Industry people. In other words,. Wynton Marsalis was ordered by computer,. but Jameel Moondoc was all me. The Industry people paid for and owned space in the store,. and I was obligated to take care of that for them. It was never a coincidence that someone had a record released, was on the cover of downbeat, and had a week at the Blue Note, all at the same time. That's good business, and also powerful. I was not without recourse however,and I had space right on the new release racks and special feature displays where I could push anybody in Jazz.I also had a budget to order product the industry people would not.I spent thousands of dollars for the store this way bringing product into the store.(An easy joke could be made here that I was part of the reason Tower fell,. and I was accused of this by a rabid Pat Metheny fan who was really angry that I Totally neglected his catalog.)

Wait a minute, . . . Pat Metheny SELLS,. and I CHOSE to NOT bring him in the store?!

That's right.I was in more interested in giving people exposure in a major store that never would give them a chance to be seen otherwise.Most of the time it wasn't personal,. I just wouldn't think of having Pat's section filled out because his music never hit me,. but sometimes I really just said no.There was 2 other people I did this to,. Eric Alexander,and Bill Charlap.I had an argument every day with one of my supervisors who LOVED Eric Alexander.He insisted that Eric was one of the greatest players around and should be featured up front,. and I insisted that he had over 20 records out that all sounded the same,and without Dexter and Coltrane he wouldn't exist his concept was so deeply rooted in theirs.

Thus,. I clearly did not make some people happy and also was taking a business risk,. but this was a rare opportunity to really turn people on from a musicians perspective,. and as many people know,. I consider all the jazz categorized as "free",. as part of jazz history. Thus,. one of the first things I did was a make a Roy Campbell jr display to promote his record,. Ethnic stew and Brew.Yes,. TAZZ is a friend of mine,made a great record,and I was going to put the public on notice they should check it out.We sold many more of those than if it was just in the bin,. and many people became fans of Roy,. came back and got a bunch of his other records,. I kept the bin filled.Featuring folks with a similar vision is no different than what Wynton does at JALC,and what people in NYC do when they book the Stone,. (one of our last viable performance spaces).If I got the gig at JALC,. yes,. Giuseppi Logan takes the MAIN.STAGE.

The 2 CD's that SOLD like crazy where the discovered Monk and Coltrane concert,. and also the discovered Bird and Diz concert. That says a great deal about jazz that the sales on those just CRUSHED everybody ALIVE. I had full displays of both Cd's and sold hundreds of them,. (a lot for jazz) . . . they are great records,. in fact Dizzy was really on FIRE during the live show,. live jazz is the best for me.

What really put my Tower jazz thing over the top was my performance series. In an unprecedented move,. my manager allowed me to book a show every Saturday at 1:00,. and he bought a sound system and CATERED IT. For about a year and a half I had Live performances and booked it myself. When Tower fell,. I HAD IT BOOKED FOR ANOTHER YEAR AND A HALF EVEN THOUGH EVERYONE PLAYED FOR FREE. That's how it was in NYC just 4 years ago.

I had over 200 consignments,(CD's people made on their own,. and then we sold for a cut). Mostly Jazz singers. When we went bankrupt,. I had to call everybody on the down low and say,. "come and get your shit,. and quick!",. because the liquidators were trying to claim EVERYTHING.(An evil couple from Texas that reminded me of George and Laura Bush)

Anyway,. the whole Tower thing could be a book that I hope somebody writes someday,. It was a different CULTURE and a different way of life. The music business was VERY different then,. just a few years ago. Thanks Internet,. and thanks IPOD. We had LISTENING STATIONS,. (remember those?),. and having my CD Spiritual Power on the new release rack next to Joshua Redman was VERY cool . . . (hah!). Many of the CD's we had in the store will never be seen again. Like many records that never got re-pressed,. they are GONE,. forever. HILTON RUIZ was booked the Saturday after he was murdered in New Orleans,. which really tore me up as we had become friends.

Great memories include the performances,. some that I was in,. mostly not . . . Ray Mantilla,(correcting 2 woman clapping out of time!),played a great set.

Playing with Sabir Mateen's Shapes, Textures, and Sounds. We did NOT hold back,. with the audience seating on a row of benches RIGHT on top of us.

Playing with Ras Moshe and hearing the extreme high register on trumpet and just SCREAMING. I don't always play like that,. but here I was in charge of jazz in the store, getting paid to just reach for the impossible, . . . it was a trip.

Steve Swell and Charles Waters with their bands, . . . both guys played VERY aggressive sets. I was always a little afraid I would push it to far,. but Steve and Charles weren't afraid and they really went for it.

Matthew Shipp. Matt played solo on our stand up,. and for me it's my favorite musical moment while working at Tower. Matt,. did not.hold.back., and he silenced the room. It was packed,. and I'll never forget looking at the audience and seeing them completely absorbed in the music. For most of the people there,. they had never heard his music,. or even any kind of Jazz outside the box,. and they were really into something new,. and digging it. People there knew they where in the musical world of an original master,. and it helped me actually gain a little more respect for the average listener seeing we could find common ground.

I in fact made a record at this series,. "Daniel Carter and Matt Lavelle at Tower",. a series of duets including me having a discussion with somebody in the audience about what kind of jazz we play,. (It's on Antnimara records)

But my favorite Tower Jazz memory is from an employee that worked with me,. who's name I respectfully withhold. I'll call him KIRK.

Kirk would TELL OFF anybody even asking about smooth Jazz . . .

"Hi, . . . Do you have any Smooth Jazz?"

"That's not the REAL thing man ..."

"What?, ... I came here to buy some smooth Jazz ..." (agitated)

"Well,. I don't have time for that bullshit ...!"

"WHAT? I didn't come here to be insulted!!"

As the manager,. I should have intervened,. but the musician in me froze up,. and I let it play out.

Just this once, ... we'll let the world KNOW how we feel ..."

Giuseppi Logan and the fall from Grace

Much has been written online,much of it by myself,about my good friend Giuseppi Logan. On youtube there's a string of videos by Suzannah B.Troy,and a documentary about the reunion of Giuseppi Logan with his son Jaee.When Henry Grimes resurfaced he was quickly put on major festival stages and eventually found an actual career as a Jazz musician. It seems that the world has a different plan though for G.

After we were able to get Giuseppi to make a record,which he did mainly to get the bread,as he was homeless at the time,things started to turn a little.G found a stable situation and was practicing everyday in the park near his room on the lower east side of NYC.Giuseppi always talked about work.He felt that all he needed to do was get some gigs and the rest would take care of itself.

Giuseppi had trouble getting the music happening,so I got him as many concerts as I could. He was practicing,getting better,day by day.We had some good ones:at 5C,(STILL holding on after long term attempts to evict them),and the STONE:maybe the only place left in NYC that isn't PAY TO PLAY.The Stone happened only because I called up John Zorn,who booked Giuseppi literally in a matter of minutes.

Giuseppi played maybe the concert of his life in PHILLY.Every time I go there they SCHOOL NYC on what a real Jazz audience is.They humiliate NY by turning out,listening really hard,and knowing the music.The place was PACKED,and even Downbeat,(sometimes known as beatdown),and the major Philly press came out.G played his ass off.Nobody in NY has ever heard him get down like this.G was trying for impossible ideas and MAKING them,. the real thing.The people really loved Giuseppi and the applause went on and on,. a personal triumph for him.Then it was back to NY.

I got the gig booking University of the streets in May, and I of course booked G. As per our usual routine, I went to go find G and bring him to the gig. I called his "residence". Giuseppi however, had decided to write the next chapter of his life a tragic one, without letting me know he had broken our deal: to keep playing music no matter what happens.

I was told on the phone that "I needed to come down right away",. as "something had happened". I was left with the impression that Giuseppi had finally decided to head home. Maybe he had heard Louis Armstrong sing "They Say I Look Like God".

I rushed to his place to then be told G was alive, but I would not be told where he was, or what his condition was.

IT WAS ON.

But I Lost . . . Bad. I demanded to know what his health was and where he was, but the staff refused without legal consent to release information from Giuseppi himself. I started a scene in this place out of anger and the director came out, pissed I interrupted his lunch, and started screaming LAW. Ready to call the POLICE. His "social worker" came out and wouldn't help at all. This guy HAD NO IDEA GIUSEPPI WAS A MUSICIAN OR HAD ANY FAMILY. HE COULD NOT CARE ANY LESS.

I canceled the gig of course and called my peeps at the Jazz Foundation, as I was headed to Italy at the end of the month. Just before I was to leave I found Giuseppi at a local hospital under the name Joe Logan. He had broken his hip and was refusing surgery. Giuseppi could not walk, and the state made a big threat: Take the surgery or we take your room and send you back to a mental home. I called the Jazz Foundation again,. surely they would be able to straighten this out.

When I got back to NYC the Jazz Foundation told me they have been jammed up by the same legal information shit. Only a Fax, signed by Giuseppi, would allow any of to help. This was now sick and ridiculous, just like MINGUS used to sing.

Now,nobody knows where Giuseppi is even at or his condition.One thing for sure,. he's not playing music.Want to start some shit?

Call that "residence" at <u>1-212-533-3737</u>.

I wish I could call Frederick Douglass.I bet he would fix this mess.Maybe Help Me Howard will have to suffice in 2011.He gave G $200 once on TV.

I also wish I could try a Nihilism perspective,but it's against my nature.

I could dig that maybe nothing means anything.Is that Buddhist? I like the idea that between lives we really find that our experiences living have no karma or consequence as long as we have learned or evolved.

But being a human being means your gonna FEEL something based on your actions and choices in life.The SOUL will let you know when something MEANS something.

When people allow things to happen that are wrong,. when they feel and know it's wrong but allow it anyway for personal gain,out of fear,or because they just don't care,. then they turn their back on themselves and what it means to be human.If are we ever to grow,we have to find the strength and courage to simply do what we know inside know is right. Giuseppi Logan himself has suffered from choices and consequences more than anybody I know.I have to think his choice to pick up an alto and play it to be a good decision,a necessary one.Must so many Lives in Jazz be filled with tragedy?

The last time I saw G he was stuck at Beth Israel hospital watching a loop on TV as he had no $ to have even basic cable turned on in his room.The loop was a never ending video of waves crashing into shore at dusk.Just what kind of message are they trying to send?

Don't write this last chapter without me man.

SMOKIN' THAT KRYPTONITE

Some people are city.Some country.Some street.Some sweet.

Like many people,I adapt to my environment.One thing Wynton Marsalis said that I like:

"It's not where your from,it's where your at."

Like Archie Shepp said on Attica Blues,.

"Where's that driving music man that used to wail out back?"

"Never knew where he came from,. a castle or a shack"

If you ever watch LIKE IT IS,with Gil Noble on Sunday mornings,you will almost always learn something.Gil loves Jazz,having Max Roach and Jackie Mac as guests.I was shook watching a rerun of one of his earliest shows from when I was about 3 in the early 70's.Gil had on a guest who proclaimed:

"The Gentrification of New York City is at hand."

REALLY? That long ago this shit was in the works?

I only bring this up of course because it's IN MY FACE at the moment.I watched Hell's Kitchen turn into Chelsea when I lived on 50th and 10th.It's about 85% done.I thought I was safe from this up in the Heights though,. Washington Heights.There's people up here who wont speak to you unless you come with Spanish.I always thought the heights would somehow be protected from gentrification,as it's such a part of the culture of NYC.

I thought wrong,as my block has been over run with COPS as if they had a known cop killer somewhere up here.We went from zero cops to about FORTY foot patrolling cops,who are just staring at EVERYONE.The slightest bit of weirdness and you better have ID.I got asked for ID the other night trying to buy a Tuna sandwich.

My man ROELFIO who owns the place I rent a room from is OK with them though.I asked him in Spanish what he thought,and he said the cops were OK,. here to protect us.He just has a different perspective.The only time he gets twisted is when the JEHOVAH WITNESS folks WAKE us up for CONVERSION on Sunday mornings.I told them to debate me without the BIBLE which left them ADRIFT.My fear is that in about 5 years,. Washington Heights will simply no longer exist.I think I have a valid concern by simply looking at HARLEM,and the knowledge that Time Warner cable just BOUGHT MINTON'S PLAYHOUSE.WTF?. What will become of our beloved jazz? I've been told not to worry as it's been preserved at Lincoln Center.

No one is free from the culture police either.I just heard Facebook called TRACEbook.A public opinion these days can get you LIT UP.I myself once was attacked online by several people afraid to reveal their actual names to me.A friend of mine hipped me to the fact that we are now amongst THE INTERNET GENERATION.I never thought about it,but here I am living my life out online.At least anyone reading this knows it's MATT Lavelle,. the guy who has Grammar madness and uses CAPS to publicly therapize himself.

I caught it again by having a public opinion at my job in Times Square.By giving my opinion of the state of the tenor in 2011,I was Cyber-lashed as a stunted burnout,angry,loud Jackass.I guess that's an opinion to,as I would hate that to be a FACT.Sales of Orchestral instruments are down by the way.After watching Tower close I should be more paranoid than I actually am about this stuff,but I'm starting to accept what I have been writing about for a long time:The Cultural destruction of New York is at hand.

When CASH truly rules,culture is simply a tool to GET MORE Cash.Jazz hasn't made money in decades,(except for industry created leaders ... maybe).Jazz is now only relevant in New York if your using it to get paid at Birdland, or your in one of Paul Motions bands at the Village Vanguard and get to play music for seemingly interested tourists. Most Jazz tourists don't care who is playing as long as they get "the NYC Jazz experience". Sometimes they show up at avant or free shows and get pretty confused. My month curating University of the Streets was Rough, so I'm writing with a slight bitter taste. I can wash it down though by writing.(heh)

It's not all bad. The Vision Festival played again, but folks are worried how long they can keep going. The UNDEAD thing is happening. NYC still has some of the greatest Jazz musicians in the world here. The music left home though,. long ago. I missed the whole Vision Festival this year as I was in Italy. In realms of culture Italy is a TREE, and America is an ACORN.

Sometimes though,. I still see things I only would in New York.

I was walking with my friend Drew, a great alto player and street musician in times square. We passed by a guy dressed as Superman.

SUPES however was skin and bones. Tore up Half cape,. and on his chest he had clipped on a piece of paper with a scribbled S. Supes was asking for change since no tourists wanted photos with him.

Drew said,.

"Man ..."

"Looks like Superman's been smoking that KRYPTONITE again."

SIR HILDRED HUMPHRIES

Man, . . . do I miss my man, . . . Sir Hildred Humphries . . .

Hildred, . . . or HUMP as I sometimes called him, . . . was and still is my connection to the SWING era. I don't have to envision what it was like, . . . or ask ken burns to ask Wynton to talk about that time like it was yesterday, . . . because not THAT long ago,. (The 80's).I was not only playing with Hildred Humphries, . . . but I was his friend.

Who's Hildred Humphries?

Well, . . . let me tell you, . . . Hildred was a sax man who played with Billie Holiday for 6 months ("the best 6 months of my life", . . . everyone said she was difficult, . . . but not with me, . . . it was a real pleasure working with her".) Hildred was also a man who played with Count Basie, . . . but got tired of the road. "When I told Basie I was tired of the road, . . . he went out and got me a gold plated tenor to get me to stay!!!, . . . I stayed a little longer, . . . but my wife convinced me to come home.".Hildred and Roy Eldridge used to practice together when they were teenagers. "Man, . . . Roy wasn't ripping like we all know him to then, . . . but he was all ready powerful enough to take out almost anyone, . . . he all ready had that combative spirit!".

Hildred was from Pittsburgh, . . . and he had a brother, . . . Frank "Fatman" Humphries, . . . a trumpet legend. They had a jazz-brothers team for many, many years. I'll never forget when I found a copy of Frank playing on a cd and went to Hildred's so we could check it out. ("Man!, . . . that's him! that's him!) Frank had passed some 10 years earlier when I was rollin' with Hildred. Let me tell you, . . . frank was B.A.D. Frank could out Maynard Maynard, . . . and I've got the track to prove it. Frank was combative like Roy Eldridge, . . . and when I met

Doc Cheatam and mentioned Frank, . . . Doc almost fell out his chair!!. When I told him about Hildred, . . . doc said, . . . "Tell him to come see me right away".

Anyway, . . . I used to go by Hildred's house when I was living in Nyack New York, . . . I went by there all the time. Sometimes We would just hang out, . . . watch tv, listen to music, . but mostly I went over there to play. Just the two of us. Hours and hours of playing standards, . . . and the blues. We played c-jam blues at least 50 times, . . . (Ive got cassettes of these sessions). Hildred was playing tenor then. Hildred would get some gigs and we would hit it, . . . Body and Soul, . . . Lester Leaps In, . . . Solitude, . . . Over the Rainbow. Hildred was a great singer to, . . . and "What a Wonderful World", . . . the Louis Armstrong joint, . . . was his signature tune. Every now and then he would break out a spiritual like Amazing Grace and leave people in tears. Hildred showed me in person that the FEELING IS THE MOST IMPORTANT THING.

HOW HE FELT THEN, . . . AND HOW I FEEL NOW.

That's how I learned what swing was all about, . . . FROM THE SOURCE.

Hildred wasn't somebody I can dream about knowing, . . . like all those people on Ken Burns talking about Sidney Bechet like they knew him personally and shit, . . . he was a real person, . . . and a treasured friend ill always miss.

My main memories of Hildred are two things.

When he talked about John Coltrane . . .

(Hildred could play Trane's countdown solo note for note!!!!)

"He's one of us, . . . some people are trying to say otherwise, . . . but I'm here to tell you, . . . John Coltrane is one of us, . . . and he might be the greatest of us".

Seeing somebody from that time tell me in person that what Trane was doing was part of jazz, . . . part of jazz history, . . . has made a HUGE impression on me. I believe that Trane's music TO THE END is JAZZ. The real thing, . . . not Ken Burns version of death.

My second biggest memory is the one ill always remember with the most feeling, . . . :

The times Hildred made me breakfast . . .

I went over there on a Sunday just to say hello and Hildred made me sit down while he made me a serious soul food breakfast. I can remember that happening several times, . . . and his lady, . . . one time she made a VICIOUS sweet potato pie.

Ive got other memories to, . . . driving Hildred to the Wiz to get a boom box in my busted ass red truck, . . . and also, . . . Hildred's big ass Cadillac!, . . . which I nicknamed "the hump-mobile". Hildred was really something else.

LOVE OF MUSIC ALLOWS PEOPLE TO CROSS ALL CULTURAL AND GENERATIONAL BOUNDARIES

Reflecting on where I got my start in jazz is in no way part of the crypt keeper vibe that is like a sickness in jazz today, . . . but more of an affirmation for myself that Ive been blessed throughout my life to have a direct connection to jazz history, . . . and that no-matter how "out" or "free" I may be perceived, . . . what I'm doing is playing jazz, . . . and I'm not playing what people might "think" jazz is, . . . and I'm not playing what Lincoln center has decided jazz is.

I'm playing the REAL thing, . . . taught to me by REAL, LIVING, . . . people.

God bless, . . . sir, . . . Hildred Humphries . . .

Nature's Wrath and Beyond

Standing on the sales floor in Times Square at Sam Ash this week waiting for a chance to either sell tourists reeds or sell somebody a $6,000 Saxophone so I can eat,I heard a voice behind me that could only be one person on Earth . . .

"LAVELLE."

Brother DC.Daniel Carter was in the house,and paying me a rare visit at work.Daniel came by to drop off a copy of his music that we are going to play this Saturday at University of the Streets.The Deeper agenda however,was an assessment of the world at large in great detail,to get as real with possible with just about everything we can think of that's important not just for us,but for the world.We spoke for almost 2 hours.When 2 free Jazz musician writer philosophers meet at the crossroads of the world,. it's ON right on you dig.

No stone,. was left unturned.

First I mentioned that before work I have been listening to Phil Schapp's Bird Flight on WKCR.Phil was playing an actual recording of BIRD doing a Listening test with writer,critic Leonard Feather.Bird listened to Johnny Hodges play Passion Flower.The music is one of Hodges brightest moments,and perhaps his most personal statement.What struck me was Birds EMOTIONAL reaction.

After a silent pause,Charlie Parker said . . ."That was Johnny Lilly Pons Hodges.You know what's so great about this is that he can SING man.

The emotion that Bird placed on the word SING.SAANG . . . left me struck. What a great signpost and validation to hear from the source of one the greatest musicians in jazz how important that was. Going deeper it reveals that of all the people who think the world begins and ends with BOP, this group does NOT include Bird himself, their hero and idol as creator. Bird went on to say that he was all about MUSIC, not categories. I have always read that Bird felt trapped by Bop and loved Classical music, and wouldn't even put down country music. Daniel and I agreed,. this proves what we thought. BIRD WAS A UNIVERSAL CAT. If he lived, he would have gone on to explore way more than bop. His string project was a signal. Ornette took his evolution and used it to evolve Jazz even further.

Next we discussed the complete destruction and devastation of Joplin Missouri. I cant front,. it has me shook. I told DC that I had spent quite an amount of time writing about how nature would CLEAN us if we kept our wide level arrogant superficial shit up. I wrote that my own conclusion of 2012 was that it might be when nature had finally had enough. Since I wrote that, suggesting a Hurricane category 8 might straighten us out, Haiti suffered one of the worst earthquakes in history, Japan had their Tidal Wave, and seemingly everyday Tornadoes have been CLEANSING the Midwest and the south.

That's just what we have to figure out. If Nature is to BREAK the world to begin anew, how is it that specific areas are destroyed? Or is it simply a fact that these places are there when nature finally loses control and at long last becomes herself? Joplin being destroyed is almost like, . . . like . . .

Like it was TARGETED.

D.C. suggested that governments may have been trying to control nature for some time now, for their own evil purposes. That leads to the people that say 9/11 was an inside job and beyond. That's truly some revolutionary thinking. If the government has even considered the idea of controlling the weather, we may be doomed as a race. Revolutionary thinking is just like revolutionary playing, and in free jazz we have been known to get our SCREAM on. Do Volcanoes SCREAM when they ERUPT?

As D.C.,said,. "Sometimes that's all you can do.Sometimes that's all we have left."

Engaging the world like that,is why I came so close to getting a TENOR a few years ago,until I was able to see that wasn't my path.

Not.Yet.

Our exploration of Tornado alley led us to explore just why it's so difficult for us to overcome the simplest concepts.

Seemingly,the human race is unable to rise above 3 simple things:

1-Being separated by RACE

2-Being separated as men and woman,and then being injected with SEXual desire

3-having MONEY

Oh yeah . . . POLITICS,RELIGION.and GREED tend to um,. cOmPllcAte shizzle . . . I mean shit.Everything and anything to control the people.Just what is the FEAR or AGENDA behind that? Why do we fall in line so easily as our TV's instruct us to do?

I mentioned how much I enjoyed what I called OBAMA's Triple play.Providing the birth certificate,roasting Trump in person,and then "killing" Bin Laden.What a Chess player! DC mentioned his belief that both Republicans and Democrats are both evil.Just more drama for us to tune into.

Are we that simple? I suggested that the creator is an interesting being to give us life and then see if we deserve to exist.Is Earth school a big test,and are we entering the finals?

DC added an idea that he read about,how everyone on Earth falls into 2 categories:

Passive submissive VS Dominant aggressive.Food for thought! (FOOD,my greatest weakness)

As we change directions in Music,sometimes provided by Miles Davis,we went back to discussing music.Like Daniel,I cant resist the sound colors of more than one horn.We just cant let it go.Like ideas,we have to explore sound perspectives.I tried to explain to both him and myself about my SYNESTHESIA.How I see a DEEP DARK RED when I hear the Alto Clarinet.I recently traded in range for sound.I told Daniel I recently had a further breakthrough in my horn family.Here it is:

Cornet=Brightness=the SUN=LOUIS influence

Flugel=Darkness=the MOON=MILES influence

Music has never stopped helping me understand myself and the world,and this recent discovery of self helps me to be honest with my true musical self.That kind of thing must be why I'm attracted to other horns:I can learn about myself through them! Want to really immerse yourself in the lesson of spiritual power and talk to the world? TRANE and ALBERT played Tenor.Tenor players are my favorite musicians on Earth.Of thousands of them,I know a few who can actually WALK the TALK.(Not just the bar.)

Daniel and I talked about many other "in house" issues not meant for the Internet.Before We went back to our paths,which cross again this Saturday,I told him this.

"Before either one of us check out,what I hope for is that in our twilight we can look around and at least see that some PROGRESS was made.All we can hope for is that the world is a little bit better than we when we came in."

"Amen to that man."

A. MEN.

A Visit from the Moon Mandala

For many moons now,. I have experienced such extreme,lucid,dreams,. that I have to refer to them as visions.

They are SO real,. I believe they are happening so completely,. that I often wake and continue the reality of the dream.When I find myself awake in the dark in my bed,. reality makes no sense.Where am I since I was just living an entirely different life in another world?

What can be troubling,. trembling,. is that these visions often bring messages and have a theme.That theme is almost always change happening not for me,. but for the entire human race,. on such a vast scale that the laws of reality as we know them will no longer apply.After all,. in these visions the laws of reality are broken so completely that I have to believe we will one day transcend our self imposed limitations.If we can grow up,. we might actually be very powerful.Even though I've been living this way a long time,and spent years working on astral travel,. I still have basic fear issues like so many human beings.Regardless, . . . "Time" is up.There's been long term questions about the human race,questions that have lasted for thousands of years,. that, . . . guess what,. are about to get answered once and for all.(cue:Nina Simone:Consummation) MmMmMmMm

DREAM FLASHBACK:

I'm in Ornette Coleman's place downtown and he has a strip of giant windows.We're talking about crop circles and I pull open the huge curtains to reveal not the street below,. but the OCEAN.

WE ARE IN THE MIDDLE OF THE OCEAN.

"Lets go to the roof and try to figure this out", . . . (Ornette)

Up on the rooftop,. 1 flight of stairs and 1 simple door,. we see that his place has been transported to the middle of the ocean,. about 10 feet above it. The Sun is bright, winds are calm, and we are surrounded by Billions upon billions of gallons of water.

"What do we do? How can we live here?" (Ornette)

We discussed our options and the last thing OC said was about "emotion-tone", when I found myself in Washington Heights in the dark around 5am.

VISION FLASHBACK, . . . about 7 hours ago.

I'm standing in a crowd of people looking up at the sky,. it's daytime but the Moon is out,. and MUCH closer than it's supposed to be. The moon is so close,. the gravity should destroy the Earth,. but we are in a place of quiet and peace.

Suddenly,. the entire surface of the moon changes to a MANDALA.

?????!!!!!!!!

What? I turned to a man next to me,. an African cat,. and asked, . . . "Do you see that? What does this mean?"

He was very calm,. and said he of course saw it,. but was not concerned. It wasn't a threat,. but a message from nature.

"It would seem,. he said,. that the changes coming to Earth are total, complete, and absolute. It's no longer a question of how or why,. it's simply a matter of WHEN."

He seemed pretty calm about it,. and then the surface of the Moon changed again into a giant GATEWAY.

"Time to go", . . . he said,. smiling at me.

These 2 visions were pretty light as my usual scenario is that the changes are about to occur,. and I have to be away from danger,. or the changes have just happened and I have to figure out the new reality and how to live, . . . kind of like being a baby,. with no family,. and no foster home. Being a baby in the middle of the desert, yet self-aware of where I came from. (This is a good case why we don't remember our past lives). Many of my dreams are from lives I have all ready lived,. or I get messages from someone I've all ready been,. taking family to a whole new level. I'm closer to them when I sleep,. we all are. The barrier between here and there gets thinner every day. No matter what happens here,. I always get a great deal of support from this place, and have for years, ever since I read Seth Speaks, by Jane Roberts.

You know this place,. the one we came from and the one we return to. The picture included is of 2 busts that my Grandfather made. Beethoven and Dr. Rev. Martin Luther King,. his heroes.

Perhaps all 3 of them are sitting down to lunch on a sunny day in the middle of the ocean under the biggest Moon Mandala anyone could possibly perceive.

*   *   *

To close NYC SUBWAY DRAMA and BEYOND,. I'll leave this Bonus track: The story of my first meeting with a good friend of mine. Thanks for spending time with me. I plan to keep writing. At least two more books and a zillion blogs before I move to the mountains, or maybe to Mars.

RATS

NYC Rats are like no other creature in the world. I don't know why there has been no documentary on them,. or even an interview attempt. Call them what you will,. disgust you they may,. these guys got Soul,. and there street wise on an a VERY high level. You may as well picture them wearing little PIMP clothes. Everybody has rat stories in NYC,. or has seen them in action.

First thing is that they RULE the subway,. anytime,. day or night. Look down in the tracks and there goes one doing his thing,. exploring every last inch of the tracks for something he can use. When the train comes,. they always have a place to go,. and they always make it. Rats aren't restricted to the tracks though, they will come right up on the platform and IGNORE you,. with a higher agenda. Ive never seen one afraid of me,. there so focused on what they want,. were just distractions. For example,. at the 50th st E stop the other day,. I saw 2 rats chasing each other up on the platform,. what were they up to? I found out about 2 minutes later when they started straight MAKING LOVE right there. Right on the platform in front of us was some BOLD shit . . .

Then there's that time the news broke that story when the rats TOOK OVER a KFC on 3rd street,. right near the blue note. They had film footage of inside the KFC,. shut down by the city, . . . where the RATS were just all over the joint . . . Some were sleeping,. some partying, . . . some were working out, . . . push-ups, . . . chin-ups and shit, . . . they just owned that joint.

Living on 50thst and 10thave,. right next to a rehab,. in NYC, . . . there's a bike path nearby that goes down to Hudson river park,. right near the World Trade Center site. I like to ride down there round midnight,. as the park is almost always deserted,. except for the stray jogging addict,. leftovers from lovers lane,. a "security" guy on his celly,. or a fisherman who never catches anything,. (who would want to from that skanky river?).Either way,. last night I found myself totally alone in a city of millions,. or so I thought,. as I was shocked to see a RAT stroll right up to me like I wasn't even there,. and park himself at the edge of the bench looking out at the water just like me.

Rat: "Nice night tonight huh?"

Me: WTF? what you mean man, . . . your supposed to be a dirty so n so who's looking to eat some trash.

Rat:, . . . "What? I cant live to? I don't get to enjoy life either? Come on man,. We have to learn to share with one another,. I got kids to provide for,. I have stuff I got to do.Cant I take a break to?"

Me:, . . . Well, . . . hey, . . . I suppose it's hard for everybody these days, . . . taking a pause down here at night kind of cools me out . . . you to?"

Rat:, . . . Yeah man, . . . I feel like I gotta look for stuff 24/7, . . . I can never stop,. I don't sleep right, . . . looking out at the water, . . . full moon, . . . relaxes me to.Its "anti-stress" and all that.

Me: "You know I ain't got no food right?"

Rat, . . . (Irate) "Man, . . . fuck you, . . . we ain't always about coping your food or whatever,. how about we just sit here and enjoy the view . . ."

Me: "OK, . . . man, . . . no dis-respect, . . . lets just cool out, . . . and cool out . . ."

Rat: "That's whats up, . . . my name is Scruts(Screw-oots), . . . short for Scrutiny,. cause I leave no stone unturned",.

Me: "Cool man, . . . my name is Matt, . . . sometimes I'm called "Cuica",. or the revered b-wood, . . . sometimes "Mattack", . . .

Rat: "4 names or personalities? Your a complex person I guess" . . .

Matt,. "Nah,. I'm just bored with my perspective."

Scruts: "You humans are never satisfied, . . . guess you want more money right?"

Matt: "That would be cool,. but . . . me, . . . I just want to tune the world" . . .

Scruts: "Sounds interesting."

Matt: "I'll tell you about it some time, . . . you might be down. Can you sing,. do you play music?"

Scruts: . . . "My brother can carry a tune, . . . I'll contact him for you".

Matt: "You,. umm,. got a cell phone or something?"

Scruts: "Working on that".

Matt: "Myspace? Facebook?

Scruts: "My son has a facebook,. I'm not into that shit. You ride your bike down here and play trumpet at night right?

I've checked you out. I'm in this area quite a bit,. so I'm sure I'll so you again".

Matt: "So,. Hows the FAM?"

Scruts: "Married life for Rats isn't really that much of a big deal commitment wise. My other son has been having some drama with the Pigeons in his block. Those damn wanna be birds get on my nerves to"

Matt: "Sky-rats."

Scruts: (a little tight and hurt) "Man,. that's COLD, . . . please don't associate me with them. (Scruts made eye contact with me here,. the one and only time he did) . . .

Me: "You've got some real insight on shit man. We should keep this dialogue going."

At this point a shadow stumbled up to us that became a person and started talking about,. I want to buy a mattress or some shit, . . . used,. WTF?, . . .

Me: "Scruts,. I gotta roll out man" . . . (Scruts knew the deal)

Scruts: "OK man, . . . peace out".

Me: (Leaving),. "Keep me updated on that Pigeon drama,. I can send some GULLS over there to straighten shit out"

Scruts: (almost smiling),. "Copy that!,. See you In a NY minute man" . . .

Later today around 1 o'clock on 50th, . . . I see a FAT rat strolling up the block,. right in time with the people traffic, . . . is he on his way to work?, . . .

"NYC RATS,. I thought,.

They are really something else."

Dedicated to the HORSES,. pulling those DAMN TOURISTS around all day, . . . stay strong brothers, . . . one day, . . . you will be FREE!!

(I have to remember to talk to Sruts this.)

PEACE